N

1 cm = 220 m   1 : 22.000

0   500   1000 m

0   0,25   0,5 mile

CITY FASHION **BERLIN**

CHRISTINE ANNA BIERHALS

CITY FASHION
BERLIN

h.f.ullmann

INHALTSVERZEICHNIS | CONTENTS

AMAZING FASHION

LUXURY FASHION

ACCESSORIES

INSIDER TIPS

Die Buchreihe CITY FASHION taucht in die faszinierende Modewelt der bekanntesten Großstädte ein. Modedesigner lassen sich aufs Neue zu innovativen Kollektionen inspirieren. Vor allem die Stadt, in der sie leben, bietet ihnen einen umfangreichen Ideenpool. Jede Metropole versprüht eine andere Mentalität und die dortige Modeszene einen eigenen Stil. In Berlin beflügelt eine Atmosphäre zwischen rasanter Entwicklung und extremen Gegensätzen, die hier zwischen Plattenbauten und glamourösem Großstadtleben herrscht, die pulsierende Kreativszene.

CITY FASHION BERLIN präsentiert verschiedenste Facetten deutscher Mode in den Teilen Amazing und Luxury Fashion und Accessoires-Design. Gezeigt werden die Upcoming-Stars, die Topdesigner und auch jene, die nur zur Fashion Week in Berlin zeigen. Damit schaut CITY FASHION BERLIN über den Tellerrand der Hauptstadt hinaus und sieht sich als Guide über Berlin als Modemetropole, die ihr Land und dessen Modeszene repräsentiert. Denn mit der hiesigen Fashion Week wurde für deutsche Designer endlich eine Plattform geschaffen, auf der sie ihre Kollektionen im eigenen Land präsentieren können.

CITY FASHION BERLIN vermittelt einen schönen Einblick in das Schaffen der Designer und verrät dem Leser den Shop in Berlin, in dem die Kollektionen erhältlich sind. Zudem geben sie ihren ganz persönlichen Hotspot in der Hauptstadt preis. Damit runden sie das Modebuch zu einem kleinen Insiderguide ab und bringen dem Leser Berlin und das dortige Lebensgefühl näher. Denn wer könnte die angesagtesten Orte besser kennen als die Insider einer Metropole, die Teil der „Szene" sind? Auf deren Spuren kann man nun neben dem Kreativvolk in den angesagtesten Bars sitzen, deren Lieblingsläden zum Shoppen auserkunden und somit ein bisschen Lebensgefühl anstatt nur Sightseeing genießen. Diese einzigartige Kombination aus einem exklusiven Einblick in das aktuelle Modegeschehen Berlins mit den Insidertipps der Designer lässt CITY FASHION BERLIN zu einem „Must Have"-Guide für Modebegeisterte und Städtereisende werden.

The CITY FASHION series dips into the fascinating world of fashion in the most well-known cities. Fashion designers find new inspiration for their inventive collections; their home town in particular offers a wealth of ideas. Every metropolis has a different mentality and bestows a unique style on its fashion industry. In Berlin, the atmosphere is a blend of rapid development and of the extreme contrasts between tower blocks and glamorous city life, so encouraging this impetuous, creative feel.

CITY FASHION BERLIN presents diverse facets of German fashion, divided into the chapters 'Amazing Fashion', 'Luxury Fashion', and 'Accessories-Design'. This book presents rising stars and established designers, as well as those who only present at Berlin Fashion Week. For this reason, CITY FASHION BERLIN looks beyond the capital's horizon and is rather a guide portraying Berlin as a fashion hub representing its country and national style. Thanks to Berlin Fashion Week, German designers can present their collections in their own country.

The book provides a stunning overview of the designers' work. It also lets the reader in on the Berlin stores that stock the collections and the artists' favorite leisure haunts, making it a handy guide for readers to discover Berlin and its lifestyle. Following their trail, you can sit in the coolest bars in town next to the creative people and discover their favorite stores, thus enjoy a little of the lifestyle rather than just sightseeing. This unique combination of exclusive insights into the current Berlin fashion scene and designers' insider tips makes CITY FASHION BERLIN a must-have guide for fashion enthusiasts and city travelers.

AMAZING FASHION

c.neeon, Fall/Winter 2009/10

KAMILA

INTRO

Das Kapitel „Amazing Fashion" präsentiert die innovative deutsche Modeszene, deren Kollektionen unterschiedlicher nicht sein könnten. Galt deutsche Mode früher einmal als rein puristisch, zeigt sie sich heute in allen möglichen Facetten von extravagant und progressiv bis hin zu schlicht, tragbar und überlegt.

Noch vor wenigen Jahren verband man Berliner Mode erst einmal mit Jungdesignern, deren selbst gestrickte Pullover und bedruckte T-Shirts mit mehr oder minder originellen Sprüchen für Unterhaltung sorgten. Mit der Gründung der Fashion Week hat sich die Hauptstadt zu einer angesehenen Modemetropole entwickelt. Die Zeit der modischen Autodidakten ist vorbei. Heute zeigen hier Designer, die mittlerweile internationale Anerkennung für ihren eigenen unverwechselbaren Stil, für Qualität und Innovation gefunden haben.

In Berlin können die Kreativen, die der Uniformität überdrüssig sind und sich nach Individualität sehnen, dem Mainstream entkommen. Die Designer in diesem Kapitel wollen sich mit ihren Kreationen sichtlich von der Masse abgrenzen. Mit experimentellen Entwürfen, neuartigen Schnitten und vielseitigen Farb- und Stoffkombinationen bringen sie neue Erscheinungsbilder hervor. Der Kreativität sind keine Grenzen gesetzt – einfach „amazing"!

„Amazing Fashion" soll Horizonte öffnen: Die folgenden Seiten bieten Kreativen, Modeinteressierten und denen, die Spaß an neuen Ideen und Innovationen haben, einen unterhaltsamen und informativen Einblick in die verrückte und kreative Welt der Mode.

The chapter 'Amazing Fashion' presents the innovative German fashion scene, with its array of highly varied collections, all different from one another. While German fashion used to be considered wholly purist, today it displays all possible facets, from the most extravagant and progressive through to the simplest, most wearable, and most sensible of styles.

Until recently, Berlin fashion was more often than not associated with young designers who set people talking with homespun sweaters and T-shirts sporting more or less original slogans. Thanks to Fashion Week, the capital has developed into a respectable fashion hub. The era of autodidacts is gone. Now designers internationally acclaimed for their unmistakable, innovative styles and the quality of their clothes, exhibit their collections here.

In Berlin the most creative designers, who reject uniformity and seek to highlight individuality, have the chance to break free from conventional fashion. The designers featured in this chapter obviously want to move away from mass production. Their experimental designs, original cuts, and blends of different colors and materials create whole new images. There is no limit to their creativity and the result is absolutely incredible —simply amazing!

'Amazing Fashion' aims to open up new horizons: the following pages offer an entertaining and informative insight into the crazy and creative world of fashion, for people who are creative-minded, for people who are interested in fashion, and for those who simply find innovation and new ideas fun.

Adddress, Spring/Summer 2011

ADDDRESS

www.adddress.de

designer | Andreea Vrajitoru

flagship store
Weinmeisterstr. 12–14 | 10178 Berlin

INSIDER TIP : CULTURE

Circleculture Gallery
www.circleculture-gallery.com
Gipsstr. 11 | 10119 Berlin

Mit ihrer Mode „adddressiert" die Designerin Frauen, die sich dezent, aber trotzdem schick kleiden wollen. Ziel von Andreea Vrajitoru ist es, eine hochwertige Tageskollektion mit leicht avantgardistischen Merkmalen zu kreieren. Damit hat sie ihren Stil auf den Punkt gebracht. Denn an ihren Entwürfen findet man keinen überflüssigen Schnickschnack. In einer unaufgeregten Lässigkeit umspielen ihre Modelle den weiblichen Körper in meist gedeckten Farben wie Schwarz, Grau oder Blau. Ihre strenge Silhouette lockert sie durch Falten und Raffungen auf, oder sie verwendet Details wie Volants oder Schleifen. Andreea Vrajitoru absolvierte ihr Modedesignstudium an der Hochschule FHTW in Berlin. Währenddessen sammelte sie erste Erfahrungen in New York bei der Designerin Anna Sui. Nachdem sie 2003 ihr eigenes Label in Berlin gründete, präsentierte sich Adddress 2009 erstmals mit einer Männerkollektion, die ebenfalls eine schlichte Handschrift trägt. Auch auf die Frage, was sie mit der Hauptstadt gemeinsam habe, antwortet Andreea Vrajitoru schlicht: „Berlin ist meine Heimatstadt. Da ist es klar, dass ich mit ihr automatisch am meisten verbunden bin."

This designer's creations are intended for the woman who seeks a discreet yet elegant style. Andreea Vrajitoru's goal is to create a collection of quality garments for daily wear, with little avant-garde touches: this is how she found the essence of her style. No superfluous accessories are to be found in her designs. Her clothes caress the female body in calm nonchalance, usually in muted colors such as black, gray and blue. Her severe silhouette is dispersed through the use of pleats and gathers, or details like flounces and ribbons.
Andreea Vrajitoru studied fashion design at the University for Applied Sciences for Technology and Economics in Berlin. She gained her early experience during this time in New York with the designer Anna Sui. After founding her own label in Berlin in 2003, Andreea presented her first menswear collection, Address, in 2009, which was also distinguished by its simplicity. When asked what she has in common with Berlin, she simply says, "Berlin is my hometown and where I grew up, so it makes sense that it's the city I feel closest to."

Artwork Helle Mardahl, Soloshow

CIRCLECULTURE GALLERY

www.circleculture-gallery.com

Gipsstr. 11 | 10119 Berlin

Die Galerie in Berlin-Mitte setzt ihren Fokus klar auf Künstler der urbanen Subkultur. Diese ziehen ihre vornehmlichen Einflüsse aus den Bereichen Streetart, avantgardistische Mode, Design und Graffitiart. XOOOOX oder Stefan Strumbel sind nur einige der bekannten Künstler, die von Circleculture ausgestellt wurden. Mit Berlin-Mitte hat die 2001 eröffnete Galerie das richtige Flair in der perfekten Umgebung für Ausstellungen dieser Art gefunden.

This gallery, located in the Berlin Mitte district of Berlin, clearly focuses on artists from the urban subculture. They draw their influences particularly from street art, avant-garde fashion, design, and graffiti art. XOOOOX and Stefan Strumbel are just two of the well-known artists who have exhibited their work at the Circleculture gallery since it opened in 2001, and which has found the perfect setting for this type of exhibition in Berlin Mitte.

A.D.Deertz, Fall/Winter 2010/11

A.D.DEERTZ

www.addeertz.com

designer | Wibke Deertz

flagship store | Torstr. 106 | 10119 Berlin

INSIDER TIP : SHOPPING

Temporary Showroom
www.temporaryshowroom.com
Kastanienallee 36 | 10435 Berlin

Umzugshelferin, Fliesenlegerin, Bühnenbauerin, Barfrau – das alles sind die Jobstationen von Wibke Deertz, bevor sie 2000 damit begann, als Modedesignerin zu arbeiten. Ihr Hang zum Handfesten entstand schon während ihres Studiums der Bildhauerei. Nachdem sie anfangs auch für Frauen unter dem Namen ADD kreierte, entschied sich die Designerin 2009 dafür, sich rein auf Männerkollektionen zu konzentrieren. „Meine Entwürfe waren im Grunde immer schon unisex", sagt sie. „Durch die Spezialisierung auf Menswear möchte ich das Profil meiner Marke schärfen." Ihre Entwürfe richten sich an Männer, die sich gut anziehen, aber nicht kostümiert wirken wollen. Ihre Mode ist unkompliziert und alltagstauglich, hat aber trotzdem immer das gewisse Etwas. Das können farbige Akzente sein oder raffinierte Verarbeitungsdetails. Wibke Deertz lebt in Berlin, ursprünglich kommt sie aber aus der Stadt Schleswig im hohen Norden von Deutschland. Ihr unstillbarer Durst nach neuen Eindrücken zieht sie jedoch immer wieder an andere Orte, wo sie auch ihre Kollektionen konzipiert. Etwa in Bangkok, Buenos Aires oder Hanoi – alles Städte, die sie in ihrer Arbeit inspirieren.

Before starting off in fashion design in 2000, Wibke Deertz worked as an assistant in a removal firm, as a floor tiler, as a stage assembler, and as a waitress. She discovered a penchant for manual labor while studying sculpture. Although she originally designed womenswear as well, under the label ADD, she chose to focus exclusively on menswear collections in 2009. "My designs have always been unisex when it comes down to it," she says. "By specializing in menswear, I am trying to shape the label's style." Her clothes are targeted at men who want to dress smartly but not feel disguised. Her style is simple and suitable for daily wear, but at the same time has a certain special hallmark, which may consist of splashes of color or fine details in the finishes. Wibke Deertz lives in Berlin, but hails from Schleswing in the far north of Germany. Her incessant search for new impressions leads her to travel to ever new locations where she conceptualizes her collections. Bangkok, Buenos Aires, and Hanoi are among the cities that have inspired her work.

TEMPORARY SHOWROOM

www.temporaryshowroom.com

Kastanienallee 36 | 10435 Berlin

**TEMPORARY
SHOWROOM**

Der Temporary Showroom von Martin Premuzic ist eine Mischung aus Presse-, PR-Agentur und Shop. Ausgewählte internationale Designer wie Odeur, Sandqvist, ffiXXed oder Henrik Vibskov finden hier für zwei bis drei Saisons eine Ausstellungsplattform zum Verkauf ihrer Kollektion. Die galerieartigen Räume befinden sich mitten im Berliner Trendviertel Prenzlauer Berg. Bei der Auswahl und Präsentation der Designer legt Premuzic, früher Inhaber einer Kunstgalerie, großen Wert auf die Einzigartigkeit der Kollektionen. „I am a fashion curator", so lautet sein Motto, und das gefällt auch A.D.Deertz, Reality Studio und Boessert/Schorn, deren Kollektionen hier ebenfalls erhältlich sind.

Martin Premužic's Temporary Showroom is store, news and fashion agency all in one. A number of selected international designers, including Odeur, Sandqvist, ffiXXed, and Henrik Vibskov have a perfect platform to promote and sell their collections for two to three seasons here. The showrooms, which are like galleries, are located in the fashionable district of Prenzlauer Berg. Premužic, formerly the owner of an art gallery, focuses on the originality of the collections in the choice and presentation of the designers. His motto, "I am a fashion curator", is shared by A.D.Deertz, Reality Studio, and Boessert/Schorn, whose collections are also available here.

ANNTIAN, Spring/Summer 2011

ANNTIAN

www.anntian.de

designer | Anne Hilken, Christian Kurt

shop | KONK
Kleine Hamburger Str. 15 | 10117 Berlin

INSIDER TIP : SHOPPING

Soeur | Vintage | www.soeur-berlin.de
Marienburger Str. 24 | 10405 Berlin

Das Berliner Label ANNTIAN verschmilzt in seinem Konzept Mode mit Grafik. Seit 2007 entwerfen Anne Hilken und Christian Kurt jährlich zwei Kollektionen. Ihre Mode findet sich auf internationalen Messen in Paris, Tokio und Berlin wieder. Die Grafikdesignerin und der Modedesigner sehen Mode weniger als Trend, sondern vielmehr als Symbiose von Farben, Stimmung, Gestaltungsfreiheit und Harmonie. „Der Mensch macht Kleidung besonders, nicht andersherum", sagt das Kreativteam. Mit klaren, reduzierten und einfachen Linien liegt die Komplexität der Kollektionen im Detail. Die meisten Kleidungsstücke werden von den Designern handbedruckt oder handbemalt. So wird jedes Teil zum individuellen Einzelstück. Die geometrischen Formen, außergewöhnlichen Schnitte und die hochwertige Verarbeitung ihrer Mode erzählen eine eigene Geschichte. ANNTIAN legt großen Wert auf die ökologische Herstellung und Verarbeitung seiner Stoffe. So arbeiten die Designer vorzugsweise mit lokalen Produzenten und Herstellern aus Deutschland, Italien und Frankreich zusammen.

The combination of fashion and graphic design defines Berlin-based label ANNTIAN for which Anne Hilken and Christian Kurt have been creating two collections a year since 2007. Their designs are shown at international fairs in Paris, Tokyo, and Berlin. Anne, a graphic designer, and clothes designer Christian don't consider fashion to be so much a trend as a symbiosis of color, mood, freedom of design, and harmony. "It is the person who gives the clothes character, not the other way around," they say. The clean-cut, effortless lines of their garments transfer the complexity of their collections into detail. The designers paint or pattern most of the clothes by hand to make each piece unique. The geometric shapes, unusual cuts, and the quality of their finishes say a lot about the spirit of their creations. ANNTIAN is very concerned with environmentally friendly production and the treatment of fabrics and preferably works with German suppliers and manufacturers, although Italian and French suppliers are also used.

Left to right: Bless, N°13, 2001 | N°36, 2008 | N°41, 2011 | N°34, 2008 | N°40, 2010

BLESS

BLESS

www.bless-service.de

designer | Desiree Heiss, Ines Kaag

flagship store | Oderberger Str. 60
Backhouse, 3rd floor | 10435 Berlin
by appointment only | tel +49 (0)30 27596566

INSIDER TIP : CULTURE

Galerie Neu | www.galerieneu.net
Philippstr. 13 | 10115 Berlin

Nur weil ihre Zeichnungen 1993 bei einem Studentenwettbewerb in Paris zufällig nebeneinanderhingen, lernten sich Ines Kaag und Desiree Heiss kennen. Seit 1997 entwirft das Designerduo mit Sitz in Paris und Berlin gemeinsam Mode, Accessoires und Industriedesign der besonderen Art. Heute zählt Bless zu den wichtigsten Impulsgebern der progressiven Modewelt. Sie kooperieren mit Designgrößen wie Martin Margiela und Markus Wente. „Unsere Arbeit ist pragmatisch und bodenständig. Anstelle von Produkten sagen wir lieber Sachen dazu", so Ines Kaag. Ganz normale Gegenstände werden von Bless auf ihre Alltagstauglichkeit hin geprüft und in klarer, eigenständiger Form neu definiert. Die Arbeit der beiden Kreativen verbindet Einflüsse aus Kunst, Mode und Design. So finden sich in ihren ausgefallenen Kollektionen einzigartige Entwürfe wie Schmuck aus Kabeln und Perlen und ein Anzug für Stühle wieder. Die Bekleidungssachen namens Allroundwear, Uncool und O.Kayers sagen viel über ihre Bestimmung aus. „Es ist ein Entwurf, wie man sein Leben verbringen möchte", erklären die Designerinnen.

Ines Kaag and Desiree Heiss met in Paris in 1993 at a student design contest where their work happened to be exhibited side-by-side. The pair, who work out of Paris and Berlin, have been designing clothes, accessories, and unusual industrial pieces together since 1997. Bless is now one of the most-talked about labels on the progressive fashion scene. The duo collaborates with big fashion names such as Martin Margiela and Markus Wente. "Our work is pragmatic," says Ines Kaag. "Instead of talking about 'products', we prefer to speak of 'personal effects'". Bless also establishes the usefulness of daily implements and gives them a logical, independent twist. The pair's work is influenced by art, fashion, and design, and explains how their extravagant collections can include unique designs such as costume jewelry made from wires and pearls and a suit for a chair. The names for their lines of clothing, such as Allroundwear, Uncool, and O. Kayers, are clear exponents of their style. "Our creations resemble how we see life," they explain.

Boessert/Schorn, Fall/Winter 2010/11

BOESSERT/ SCHORN

www.boessert-schorn.de

designer | Sonia Bößert

shop | Temporary Showroom
Kastanienallee 36 | 10435 Berlin

> **INSIDER TIP** : SHOPPING
>
> **KONK** | www.konk-berlin.de
> Kleine Hamburger Str. 15 | 10117 Berlin

Das Markenzeichen von Boessert/Schorn ist ein Wappen – mit Nadel und Faden auf der linken und einem Falken auf der rechten Seite. Die beiden Hälften symbolisieren die beiden Gründerinnen: Der Vogel steht für Sonia Bößert, das Nähzeug für Brigitte Schorn. Diese stieg allerdings 2010 aus dem gemeinsamen Unternehmen aus. Die beiden lernten sich während ihres Studiums in Halle an der Kunsthochschule Burg Giebichenstein kennen. 2003 beschlossen sie, mit ihrem eigenen Label durchzustarten. Anfangs arbeiteten die Designerinnen erst einmal nebenbei daran. Mit wachsendem Erfolg steckten Boessert/Schorn ab 2006 ihre ganze Energie in ihr Projekt. Besonders in Japan kam ihr beduinenhafter Stil mit den voluminösen Formen und dem schrägen Farbmix gut an. Seitdem präsentierten sie ihre Kollektionen in Tokio, seit 2008 in Paris und seit 2010 auch in New York. Sonia Bößert, die nun das Label allein weiterführt, lässt sich von Trachten, alten Handwerkstechniken, Kunstrichtungen wie Bauhaus und Dada und vom ganz normalen Alltag inspirieren. Trotz ihres Erfolgs in den internationalen Modestädten bekennt sie sich klar zu Berlin: „Um kreativ zu arbeiten und zu leben, ist diese Stadt einfach interessanter."

The Boessert/Schorn emblem is a coat of arms: on the left is a needle and thread, and on the right, a falcon. The two halves represent the founders: the bird is Sonia Bößert, and the sewing implements, Brigitte Schorn, who left the label they had established together in 2010. The pair met in Halle while they were students at the University of Art and Design. In 2003 they decided to move into fashion, creating their own label. At first it was a sideline, but their growing success led them to turn to design full time in 2006. The Bedouin-style voluminous shapes and outlandish color mixes proved particularly popular in Japan. They then began presenting collections in Tokyo, which they followed up with shows in Paris in 2008 and New York in 2010. Sonia Bößert, who currently runs the label alone, seeks inspiration in folk costumes, old craft techniques, and art movements such as Bauhaus and Dada, but also in daily life. Despite her success in various international fashion capitals she confesses to a predilection for Berlin: "This city is the most interesting city in which to live and work creatively," she says.

Boessert/Schorn, Spring/Summer 2010

Boessert/Schorn, Spring/Summer 2010

Boessert/Schorn, Fall/Winter 2010/11

KONK

www.konk-berlin.de

Kleine Hamburger Str. 15 | 10117 Berlin

KONK

Ettina Berríos-Negrón hat genau das richtige Gespür für aufstrebende Talente. Die Besitzerin der kleinen Damenboutique rundet die Kollektionen der angesagten, jungen, internationalen Avantgardedesigner mit innovativem Schmuck und Accessoires perfekt ab. Neben den begehrten Labels der Hauptstadt wie c.neeon, kvast oder Boessert/Schorn präsentiert Berríos-Negrón, gelernte Modedesignerin, innovative Labels aus London, New York und Kopenhagen.

Ettina Berríos-Negrón has a nose for detecting new talent. Owner of a small ladieswear boutique, she excels at matching innovative costume jewelry and accessories with the collections from the most trendy and avant-garde young designers of international renown. As well as the leading labels in the capital such as c.neeon, kvast, and Boessert/Schorn, Berríos-Negrón, with her background in fashion design, she stocks hitherto unheard of labels from London, New York, and Copenhagen.

C'EST TOUT

www.cesttout.de

designer | Katja Will

flagship store | Mulackstr. 26 | 10119 Berlin

C'est tout
Berlin

INSIDER TIP : SHOPPING

Departmentstore-Cabinet | Quartier 206
www.cabinet206.com
Friedrichstr. 71 | 10117 Berlin

Die Devise der Designerin Katja Will lautet: „Alles, was eine Frau zum perfekten Look braucht, ist das passende Kleid." Dementsprechend vielseitig sind ihre Variationen: In ihren Kollektionen präsentiert C'est tout schlichte Tageskleider, aber auch glamouröse Paillettenoutfits für den Abend, Lederjacken und lässig elegante Oberteile. Im Frühjahr 2007 gründete Katja Will zusammen mit ihrem Partner Michael Will ihr Label in Berlin. Vorher arbeitete sie sechs Jahre als „Head of Style" bei MTV und agierte nebenher immer wieder als Modeexpertin für verschiedene TV-Formate. Das junge Unternehmen C'est tout setzt heute auf den Produktionsstandort Deutschland. Die Kollektionen werden ausschließlich in deutschen Manufakturen und Konfektionsbetrieben produziert. Im Winter 2010 präsentierte das Label zum ersten Mal seine Modelle auf der Fashion Week. Warum Katja Will ausgerechnet Berlin als Modestandort ausgesucht hat, begründet die gebürtige Erfurterin so: „Ich würde sonst immer ganz wehmütig auf die Menschen schielen, die in dieser wunderbaren Stadt leben dürfen."

Designer Katja Will's slogan is "Any dresses that make women look good are suitable". In keeping with the idea behind the slogan, her designs are highly varied. C'est Tout collections cover simple daywear and glamorous sequined eveningwear, leather jackets, and top-quality garments of relaxed elegance. In spring 2007, Katja created the Berlin-based label along with her partner Michael Will. She had previously worked as a style director on MTV for six years and made regular appearances on TV as a fashion expert. The young company is based in Germany and the clothes are made exclusively in this country. The label presented models at Fashion Week for the first time in winter 2010. Katja Will, originally from Erfurt, says she chose Berlin as the center of her operations because as she states "If I hadn't, I would have always been envious of the people who have the chance to live in this wonderful city."

DEPARTMENTSTORE-CABINET

www.cabinet206.com

Quartier 206 | Friedrichstr. 71 | 10117 Berlin

Im Untergeschoss des hippen Quartier 206 versteckt sich eine Schatzkammer für Modebegeisterte. Auf den 450 m² finden die rund 50 avantgardistischen internationalen Labels wie Isabel Marant, Vanessa Bruno und Acne einen ganz besonderen Platz. Neben den topmodischen Labels gibt es hier immer wieder kleine Besonderheiten wie beispielsweise eine Designlinie des It-Girls Chloë Sevigny – exklusiv designt für das New Yorker Label Opening Ceremony – zu entdecken.

The ground floor of Quartier 206, with its hippy vibe, has become a goldmine for fashion enthusiasts. In its 4,800 square feet, close to 50 avantgarde labels including Isabel Marant, Vanessa Bruno, and Acne have found a space that suits them to a tee. As well as cutting-edge labels, it is also a place to find small, unique items such as a design line by Italy's Chloë Sevigny produced exclusively for the New York label Opening Ceremony.

Clarissa Labin, Spring/Summer 2011

CLARISSA LABIN

CLARISSA LABIN

www.clarissalabin.com

designer | Clarissa Labin

shop | KONK
Kleine Hamburger Str. 15 | 10117 Berlin

INSIDER TIP : FOOD
Kantine
www.kantine-berlinmitte.blogspot.com
Joachimstr. 11 | 10119 Berlin

„Berlin kann in Bezug auf Mode noch lange nicht mit Paris oder London mithalten", findet die deutsch-venezuelanische Designerin. „Da muss noch einiges passieren." Um etwas in diese Richtung zu bewegen, zeigte Clarissa Labin im Frühjahr 2010 bei den Berliner Press Days zum ersten Mal ihre Modelle. An diesen Tagen öffnen Presseagenturen ihre Türen, um Medienvertretern die Kollektionen der Designer, die sie vertreten, vorzustellen. Die Modejournalisten mochten ihre Ideen sofort: An ihren Strickkreationen mit den dreidimensionalen Oberflächen und den ausdrucksstarken Ornamenten sahen sie auf Anhieb, dass sie keine Anfängerin mehr war. In der Tat konnte die gebürtige Hamburgerin einige Jahre Berufserfahrung sammeln: Nach ihrem Abschluss am London College of Fashion war sie ab 2000 Assistentin bei Daniel Swarovski und der britischen Vogue. Danach war Clarissa Labin in Paris als Accessoire-Designerin für Christian Dior tätig. Anschließend wechselte sie nach Stockholm zu H&M, um dort zunächst eine Linie für Strick und Jersey zu betreuen. 2006 übernahm sie als „Head of Design" das „Divided Black Label" des schwedischen Moderiesen. Heute lebt Clarissa Labin in Berlin und arbeitet von dort aus an ihrer vierten eigenen Kollektion.

"Some things will still have to change to make Berlin a fashion capital on a par with Paris or London," this German/Venezuelan designer believes. Clarissa Labin did her bit by showing her models for the first time in spring 2010 at the Berlin Press Days, where various firms present their collections to the media. The fashion journalists loved her ideas immediately. Seeing her knitwear designs with 3D surfaces and expressive ornaments, they were quick to realize she was no novice. Indeed, Clarissa, originally from Hamburg, had already accumulated a great deal of experience; after finishing her studies at the London College of Fashion in the year 2000, she began to work as an assistant to Daniel Swarovski and for Vogue in the UK. She later went on to design accessories for Christian Dior in Paris, before being taken on by H&M in Stockholm. At first she developed a line for the label Strick und Jersey, and in 2006 headed up, as design director, the Swedish fashion giant's Divided Black label. Today Clarissa Labin lives in Berlin and is working on her fourth collection.

Clarissa Labin, Moodboard, Spring/Summer 2011

JUNE DRESS ARTWORK GRAPHIC

FRONT

Clarissa Labin, Fall/Winter 2010/11

c • neeon

C.NEEON

www.cneeon.com

designer | Clara Leskovar, Doreen Schulz

flagship store | Kastanienallee 55 | 10119 Berlin

INSIDER TIP NIGHTLIFE

Picknick Berlin | www.picknickberlin.de
Dorotheenstr. 90 | 10117 Berlin

Der Labelname setzt sich zusammen aus „c" wie Clara und „Neeon" – so nannte man Doreen in ihrer Kindheit. Kennengelernt haben sich die beiden in Berlin, wo sie an der Kunsthochschule Weißensee studierten: Die gebürtige Thüringerin Doreen Schulz belegte dort den Studiengang Modedesign, die Berlinerin Clara Leskovar studierte Textildesign. Noch während ihres Studiums sammelten die beiden erste Erfahrungen bei renommierten Designern: Clara Leskovar arbeitete für das deutsch-französische Avantgardelabel Bless, und Doreen Schulz war Assistentin bei Bernhard Willhelm. Die perfekte Basis also, um im Frühjahr 2004 mit ihrem gemeinsamen Label durchzustarten. Schon 2005 konnten sie ihren ersten großen Erfolg verbuchen: Sie gewannen den Grand Prix des internationalen Modefestivals im französischen Hyères. Ihre Mode mit den grafischen Mustern und den asymmetrischen Schnitten ist heute weltweit gefragt. In den USA bezeichnet man sie sogar als „Neo-Bauhaus-Fashion". Im Frühjahr 2009 zeigten c.neeon erstmals ihre Kollektion zur Fashion Week im weißen Zelt. Heute präsentieren sie nicht nur in der Hauptstadt, sondern zudem international in Paris und Tokio.

The name of the label is formed by the 'c' for Clara and 'Neeon', Doreen's childhood nickname. The two designers met in Berlin when studying at the Weissensee School of Art. Doreen Schulz, originally from Thuringia, enrolled in fashion design, while Berliner Clara Leskovar studied textile design. Both built up experience as students working with renowned designers; Clara with the fashion-forward label Bless, and Doreen as an assistant to Bernhard Willhelm. This work experience enabled them to create their own label in spring 2004. They achieved their first big success a year later, taking home the Grand Prix award at the international Hyères Festival. Their clothes, with graphic motifs and asymmetrical cuts, have achieved international renown. Their style is even classified as Neo Bauhaus Fashion in the States. For the first time in spring 2009, c.neeon presented a collection at Fashion Week that appeared in the White Tent. Today they present in the German capital and abroad, including Paris and Tokyo.

c.neeon, Fall/Winter 2010/11

c.neeon, Fall/Winter 2009/10

PICKNICK

www.picknickberlin.de

Dorotheenstr. 90 | 10117 Berlin

PICK NICK

Der lauschig-kleine angesagte Elektro-Hinterhofclub von Björn Ney und Tanja Kreisz präsentiert nicht nur zwei kuschelige Dancefloors, sondern auch einen schönen Außenbereich. Hier lässt es sich im Sommer problemlos und ohne irgendjemanden zu stören zu guter Musik abtanzen. Die junge Berliner Kreativszene feiert hier bis in die frühen Morgenstunden. An anderen Tagen finden in dem schönen alten Backsteingebäude diverse Veranstaltungen wie Filmpremieren oder Modenschauen statt.

Björn Ney and Tanja Kreisz's small, welcoming electronic music club not only has two fabulous dance floors but also a lovely, large outdoor courtyard. In summer you can groove to the music all night without disturbing the neighbors. This is where Berlin's brightest young creative talents hang out until the early hours of the morning. Film premieres and fashion parades are also organized in this lovely brick venue.

ESTHER PERBANDT

www.estherperbandt.com

designer | Esther Perbandt

flagship store | Almstadtstr. 3 | 10119 Berlin

INSIDER TIP : NIGHTLIFE

Trust Bar | Torstr. 72 | 10119 Berlin

Nach Abschluss ihres Studiums am Pariser Institut Français de la Mode war Esther Perbandt als Designerin bei der französischen Prêt-à-porter-Linie Chacok tätig. 2003 kehrte sie wieder zurück in ihre Heimatstadt Berlin. Dort gründete sie ein Jahr später ihr Modelabel. Seitdem zeigt sie ihre Kollektion während der Fashion Week meist in „Offside-Locations", also an externen Veranstaltungsorten jenseits des weißen Mercedes-Benz Fashion Zelts: Das können Projekträume sein, Hotels oder einfach die Straße. Trotz ihres internationalen Erfolgs konnte sie sich ihren Geheimtippcharakter bewahren. Besonders in der Berliner Kunst- und Kulturszene sind ihre avantgardistischen Entwürfe beliebt. Typisch für Perbandts Stil ist ein Hauch von Androgynität, der sich wie ein roter Faden durch ihr Schaffen zieht. Ihre körpernahen Schnitte spielen mit Proportion und ungewöhnlichen Materialkombinationen, etwa Ketten und Kordeln, die oft im Kontrast zu feinen Stoffen wie Seide und Chiffon stehen. „Berlin ist ein hervorragender und nach wie vor bezahlbarer Ort, um kreativ zu arbeiten", erklärt sie. Ihr Lieblingsplatz ist trotzdem ihr Bett. Denn ihre unkonventionellen Ideen kommen der Designerin meistens im Schlaf.

Having finished her studies at the Institute of French Fashion in Paris, Esther Perbandt worked as a designer for the French line of Chacok ready-to-wear. In 2003 she returned to her native city of Berlin and a year later founded her own fashion label. Since then she has presented her collections at Fashion Week, but generally on secondary stages rather than in the Mercedes-Benz Fashion Week's White Tent: in a meeting room, a hotel, or just in the street. Despite her international success, the label has been able to maintain a confidential side. Her cutting-edge designs are particularly appreciated on the Berlin art and culture scene. Perbandt's style is characterized by a slightly androgynous feel and by the red thread that runs through all of her creations. Her body-skimming cuts play with proportions and with an unusual combination of materials, such as chains and cords, which often contrast with the delicate materials such as silk and transparent gauze. "Berlin is a wonderful city where you can work as a creator just like before and without having to get into debt," the designer says. However, her favorite place is her bed, so it makes sense her original ideas come to her when she is asleep.

Esther Perbandt, Fall/Winter 2010/11

TRUST BAR

Torstr. 72 | 10119 Berlin

TRUST

Eine Bar mit Toilettenschiebetür, die nur Flaschen und Karaffen statt einzelner Drinks anbietet, lädt zum vertrauten Miteinander mit den Tischnachbarn ein. „Ein Ort, an dem man manchmal nicht genau weiß, warum man ihn so sehr liebt: Manchmal ist er gemütlich, manchmal aufregend und wild, manchmal inspirierend und manchmal total überfüllt. Er liegt so versteckt, dass man ihn als Fremder kaum finden kann. Bei dem Getränkekonzept will jede Berliner Schnauze sofort lauthals anfangen zu meckern, gesteht sich dann aber doch irgendwann ein, dass es eigentlich interessant und neu ist. Eine Bar, der man eigentlich nicht trauen kann. Hier fühle ich mich zu Hause", schwärmt die Designerin Esther Perbandt.

A bar with sliding doors in the bathroom, where jugs and bottles are served instead of glasses, invites you to connect with the rest of the clientele. Designer Esther Perbandt is a huge fan of the venue: "There is something about it that makes you ask yourself why you like it so much. The ambiance is usually really welcoming, sometimes exciting and out-there, and occasionally intimate. It's nearly impossible to find if you're not from here because it is so hidden away. At first everyone in Berlin was complaining about the way the drinks were served, but it didn't take long for them to realize that it's a really interesting and novel idea. It is a bar where you can truly feel at home".

FIRMA

www.firma.net

designer | Daniela Biesenbach, Carl Tillessen

flagship store | Mulackstr. 1 | 10119 Berlin

INSIDER TIP : CULTURE

Contributed Gallery | www.contributed.de
Strausberger Platz 16 | 10243 Berlin

Das Designduo gehört fast schon zu den alten Hasen in der Berliner Modeszene. 1997 gründeten Daniela Biesenbach und Carl Tillessen ihre „FIRMA" – zunächst als Männerlabel, 2006 folgte die Frauenkollektion. Heute spielen die Designer mit ihrem klaren Design und den messerscharfen Schnitten längst in der ersten Liga. Ihre großen Vorbilder sind die Pioniere der Bauhaus-Bewegung, was sich auch in ihren zeitlosen Modellen widerspiegelt. Darin spielt die Farbe Schwarz stets eine dominante Rolle. Das Geheimnis ihres Erfolgs basiert nicht nur auf ihrem gestalterischen Talent, sondern vor allem auf ihrem handwerklichen Können. Beide sind ausgebildete Schneidermeister. Für FIRMA ist nichts wichtiger, als dass die Verarbeitung stimmt. „Das ist für uns der Ausdruck wahren Luxus." Ihre Interpretation haben Berliner Modejournalisten offenbar verstanden. Denn 2003 zeichneten sie FIRMA mit ihrem Kritikerpreis „Goldene Nase" aus. Die beiden Rheinländer haben bewusst Berlin als Standort gewählt. „Weil in der Hauptstadt im Gegensatz zu anderen Städten bürgerliche Statussymbole keine Rolle spielen", sagen sie. „Nerzmäntel und Perlenketten interessieren hier niemanden."

Daniela Biesenbach and Carl Tillessen are established stars in the Berlin fashion firmament. In 1997 they created the label FIRMA, exclusively for men, but in 2006 followed it with a womenswear collection. With a highly personal style and subtle cuts, the duo has already carved a name for themselves amongst the fashion greats. The timeless models, in which the color black plays a dominant role, reflect the influence of their main references; the pioneers of the Bauhaus movement. The secret of their success lies not just in their creative talent but also their tailoring skills. They are both qualified master tailors. For FIRMA there is nothing more important than something well-finished: "For us, that is where true luxury lies". The Berlin fashion press appears to share this ideal, awarding FIRMA the Golden Nase Critics Prize in 2003. The pair, both originally from the Rhineland, chose deliberately to live in Berlin and for good reason: "In the capital, unlike in other cities, the distinctive symbols of the middle class don't have the same importance. Mink coats and pearl necklaces are of no interest to anyone here," they say.

FIRMA, Spring/Summer 2011

FIRMA, Fall/Winter 2010/11

FIRMA, Fall/Winter 2010/11

FIRMA, Spring/Summer 2011

FIRMA, Illustration

FRANZIUS

FRANZIUS

www.franzius.eu

designer | Stephanie Franzius

shop | KONK
Kleine Hamburger Str. 15 | 10117 Berlin

INSIDER TIP | FOOD

Kimchi Princess | www.kimchiprincess.com
Skalitzer Str. 36 | 10999 Berlin

„Je weniger Nähte, desto besser", so lautet das Motto von Stephanie Franzius. Ihre weiten, kimono-artigen Kleider entstehen nicht, indem sie Stoffe zerschneidet, sondern sie lässt sie fließen. Für ihre Entwürfe verwendet die Designerin Seiden-gewebe aller Art: Chiffonseide, Crêpe de Chine und weiche Viskose sind oft mit abstrakten Mustern bedruckt. Am liebsten drapiert Stephanie Franzi-us an der Puppe. Das hat sie in ihrem Praktikum bei Victor & Rolf, den niederländischen Couture-Genies, gelernt. Zuvor studierte sie in Berlin, Mailand und New York, wo sie Kurse an der Parsons School of Design belegte. Ihren Masterstudien-gang absolvierte Stephanie Franzius schließlich am Arnheimer Fashion Institute. Kein Wunder, dass die Designerin mittlerweile ihr Können zur Perfektion gebracht hat. Geboren wurde sie in Darmstadt, in Berlin wuchs sie auf. „Es war nicht immer mein Traum, hier zu leben", gibt sie zu. Nach ihren zahlreichen Auslandsaufenthalten hat sie ihre Meinung jedoch geändert. Ihr Resümee nach all ihren Etappen: „Ich will in Berlin bleiben. Hier kann ich das Leben leben und arbeiten, wie ich möchte."

Stephanie Franzius's motto is "the fewer seams the better!" She doesn't create her loose-fitting, kimono-style dresses by cutting fabrics but rather by playing with their bulk, and employs all manner of soft, silky fabrics: chiffon, China crepe silk and soft rayon, onto which she often stamps abstract motifs. Stephanie prefers to drape her gowns straight onto the mannequin. She learnt this technique while doing work expe-rience with Dutch dressmaking geniuses Victor & Rolf. She previously studied in Berlin, Milan, and New York, where she enrolled in a number of courses at the Parsons School of Design. She did a Master's degree at the Arnheim Fashion Institute in the Netherlands. So it is little wonder that, with this background, she has carried her training through to perfection. Stephanie was born in Darmstadt, but grew up in Berlin. She confesses that living in the capital had not al-ways been her dream, but after various periods spent abroad she changed her mind: "I want to stay in Berlin. Here I can live and work the way I want to".

Franzius, Fall/Winter 2010/11

Franzius, Fall/Winter 2010/11

65

KIMCHI PRINCESS

www.kimchiprincess.com

Skalitzer Str. 36 | 10999 Berlin

김치공주

Bei Kimchi Princess kann man koreanische Köstlichkeiten auf rustikalen Bänken, an Holztafeln sitzend, genießen. Neben einer Auswahl an typisch koreanischen Spezialitäten und Drinks wie dem Süßkartoffelschnaps Soju oder traditionellem Tee bietet die Karte alles, was das Feinschmeckerherz sonst noch begehrt. Nach einem Essen in gemütlicher Atmosphäre kann der Abend in der Soju Bar, direkt neben dem Kimchi Princess, weitergehen. Bei guten Drinks unter kleinen koreanischen Leuchtreklamen kann es schon mal passieren, dass man das Ort- und Zeitgefühl verliert und sich mitten in Berlin auf einmal in Korea wiederfindet.

At the Kimchi Princess restaurant diners seated on rustic benches can enjoy the delicacies of Korean cuisine laid out on the wooden tables. As well as typical Korean specialties and drinks, such as *Soju*, a sweet liquor made from potatoes, and traditional teas, the menu offers everything lovers of fine food could desire. After dining in a lovely ambiance you can continue the night at the Soju Bar next door. The great drinks and the décor of luminous signs contribute to the feeling that you have been transported in time and space to suddenly find yourself, while in downtown Berlin, in the middle of Korea.

f.rau, Fall/Winter 2010/11

F.RAU

www.f-rau.com

designer | Martina Rau

concept store | Gormannstr. 7 | 10119 Berlin

INSIDER TIP | FOOD

HBC Restaurant | www.hbc-berlin.de
Karl-Liebknecht-Str. 9 | 10178 Berlin

Kreativ wie ihre Mode ist auch der Name des Labels von Martina Rau. Die Designerin wollte schon immer „fraulich" elegante Kollektionen entwerfen, die der „f.rau" von heute mit ihren Bedürfnissen und Ansprüchen gerecht werden. Das Label setzt auf besondere Verarbeitungsdetails, außergewöhnliche Schnittführung und hochwertige Materialien. Schon mit 13 Jahren entdeckte Martina Rau die Liebe zu Stoffen und begann sich ihre ersten Kleider selbst zu nähen. Jahre später zog es sie für ihr Modedesignstudium endlich nach Berlin. Nachdem Martina Rau Praxiserfahrung bei Größen wie Vivienne Westwood und Alexander McQueen sammeln konnte, rief sie 2004 ihr eigenes Label erfolgreich ins Leben. Heute ist das Label nicht nur in dem eigenen Atelier und Concept Store in der Hauptstadt, sondern auch international erhältlich. „Ich liebe Berlin, die pulsierende Stadt, die im ständigen Prozess dem Geist freien Raum zur eigenen Entfaltung und Vervollkommnung lässt. Ich finde darin meine Gestaltungsmotivation", erklärt Frau Rau.

The name of the label that Martina Rau runs, f.rau ('woman' in German), is as creative as its designs. Martina always longed to produce elegant 'feminine' collections that would meet the needs and requirements of the women of today. The label is renowned for the details in its finishes, original cuts, and good quality material. Martina Rau first developed an interest in fabric at the age of 13 and started making her own dresses. A few years later she finally moved to Berlin to study fashion design. After gaining experience with fashion greats of the likes of Vivienne Westwood and Alexander McQueen, she successfully set up her own label in 2004. Her clothes can be found in Berlin in her atelier and concept store, and also abroad. She says, "I adore Berlin. It's a vibrant capital in the midst of continual progress, but where the spirit is free enough to develop and reach perfection. Here I find the inspiration I need to create".

f.rau, Fall/Winter 2010/11

HANNIBAL

www.hannibal-collection.com

designer | Simon Hannibal Fischer

shop | Hannes Roether + concept store Berlin
Fasanenstr. 61 | 10719 Berlin

INSIDER TIP : FOOD

Michelberger Hotel
www.michelbergerhotel.com
Warschauer Str. 39 | 10243 Berlin

„Mich inspirieren Märchen. Mich fasziniert es, wie man ein Märchen erfinden und über so lange Zeit so viele Menschen damit faszinieren kann." Für die Winterkollektion 2011/12 ließ sich Simon Hannibal Fischer von Krabat, der Geschichte eines Zauberlehrlings, der sich gegen seinen Meister behaupten muss, inspirieren. Am Ende siegt die Liebe über die dunklen Mächte. Hannibal triumphiert mit der Liebe zum Detail. Die Herrenkollektionen wollen Männer nicht verkleiden, sondern ihre Individualität mit klassischen, aber modernen Schnitten und hochwertigen Materialien unterstreichen. Die Atmosphäre in dem dunklen Märchen Krabat hat der Designer in seine Mode einfließen lassen: Nebelschwaden, die in einer diesigen Waldlichtung heraufziehen, schwarze Raben. Das Ergebnis ist eine dunkle, coole Kollektion mit klaren Linien, die puristisch und doch besonders wirkt. Schwarze Capes, übergroße Strickschals und Bundfaltenhosen wirken miteinander kombiniert immer noch selbstverständlich und nicht kostümiert. Das Label produziert sozial verträglich und nachhaltig in Handarbeit in Deutschland. Hannibal sitzt zwar in München, zeigt aber in Berlin. „Wo sonst? Berlin ist die Metropole Deutschlands und repräsentiert zur Fashion Week die deutsche Modeszene", so Yvonne Perner, Marketingfrau und zweite Seele von Hannibal.

"I am inspired by stories; it fascinates me how a person can invent a story and seduce so many people with it for years". For his winter 2011/2012 collection, Simon Hannibal Fischer drew on the story *The Curse of the Darkling Mill*, which tells the tale of an apprentice magician who yearns to beat his master. In the end, love triumphs over dark powers. Hannibal himself triumphs through his love for detail. His menswear collections aim to underline a man's individuality with classic yet modern cuts and the use of high quality material. The designer's clothes embody the air of the mysterious story of *The Curse*: veils of fog that rise in a forest clearing, black ravens, etc. The result is a cool, dark collection based on well-shaped lines that emit a purist and at the same time original effect. Black capes, outsized knit scarves, and pleated trousers: instead of disguising the man, the three pieces combine perfectly. The label is artisanally produced in Germany respecting environmental and social solidarity criteria. Although the founder lives in Munich, he shows in Berlin. "Where else?" says Yvonne Perner, the head of marketing and Hannibal's right-hand woman. "Berlin is the metropolis of Germany and symbolizes the national fashion scene during Fashion Week".

Hannibal, Fall/Winter 2011/12

MICHELBERGER HOTEL

www.michelbergerhotel.com

Warschauer Str. 39 | 10243 Berlin

Michelberger Hotel

Ein Mittagessen auf einem der 100 Holzstühle im Speisesaal des Michelberger Hotels, zu dem hausgemachte Limonade gereicht wird, empfiehlt das Team von Hannibal. Bei einer begehrten, stets wechselnden Tageskarte mischt sich die Kreativszene Berlins mit Besuchern und Reisenden unter dem Glaskugelhimmel des 119-Zimmer-Hotels. Im Sommer bietet der Hinterhof eine kleine Entspannungspause. Abends lädt die gemütliche Bar zum Treffen mit Freunden oder Unbekannten ein. Ein Hotel von Freunden für Freunde, designt in poetischem Minimalismus mit Improvisations- und Recyclingaspekten.

Hannibal's team recommends enjoying lunch and homemade lemonade while seated on one of the hundred wooden seats in the Michelberger hotel. Berlin's creative movers and shakers mix with visitors and travelers around the popular and always-changing set menu under the glass dome of this 119-room hotel. In summer the rear courtyard is an ideal place to unwind. At night, the agreeable bar becomes a favorite meeting point for friends and strangers alike. It is a charming hotel with a friendly atmosphere that has a poetic minimalist design in which improvisation and recycling have found a place.

Menards in Common Spring/Summer 2011

MONGRELS IN COMMON

www.mongrelsincommon.com

designer | Livia Ximénez-Carrillo, Christine Pluess

shop | F95 Store
www.f95store.com

INSIDER TIP | FOOD

Rodeo Berlin | www.rodeo-berlin.de
Auguststr. 5 | 10117 Berlin

Die beiden Designerinnen lernten sich in Berlin auf der Modeschule ESMOD kennen. Dort fanden sie heraus, dass sie eines gemeinsam haben: einen unterschiedlich kulturellen Background. Livia Ximénez-Carrillo kommt aus Deutschland und hat spanische Wurzeln. Christine Pluess ist Schweizerin mit peruanischem Blut. Als sie dann auch noch merkten, dass sie die gleiche Designsprache sprechen, beschlossen die beiden 2006, ihr eigenes Label zu gründen. Der Name war schnell gefunden: „Mongrels in Common", was so viel heißt wie „Ein Mischling zu sein – das ist unsere Gemeinsamkeit". Er hätte nicht treffender sein können, denn auch in ihren Entwürfen mischt das Kreativteam munter drauflos: verschiedene Epochen und Kulturen, den Stil der 1960er- und 1980er-Jahre, Sexyness und Biederkeit. Ihr Debüt feierten sie noch im gleichen Jahr im Rahmen des Moët & Chandon-Fashion-Awards. Ein Jahr später wurde ihre Männerkollektion mit dem „Premium Young Designers Award" ausgezeichnet. Mittlerweile konzentrieren sich die Designerinnen ausschließlich auf ihre Frauenlinie.

These two designers met at the ESMOD fashion school in Berlin. There they discovered they had something in common, their different cultural backgrounds. Livia Ximénez Carrillo is German, but of Spanish origin. Christine Pluess is Swiss with Peruvian blood. When they realized they also shared the same ideas about fashion, in 2006 they decided to create their own label. It wasn't hard to come up with the name 'Mongrels in Common', because, as they say, "being from mixed racial backgrounds, that is our common feature". Indeed, the name couldn't be more fitting, as the duo is fearless about mixing styles in their designs: bringing together different ages and cultures, combining the styles from the 1960s and 1980s; uniting the sensual with the chaste. They debuted at the Moët & Chandon Fashion Award that same year. The next year saw them take home the Premium Young Designers award for their menswear collection. The two designers now concentrate exclusively on their womenswear line.

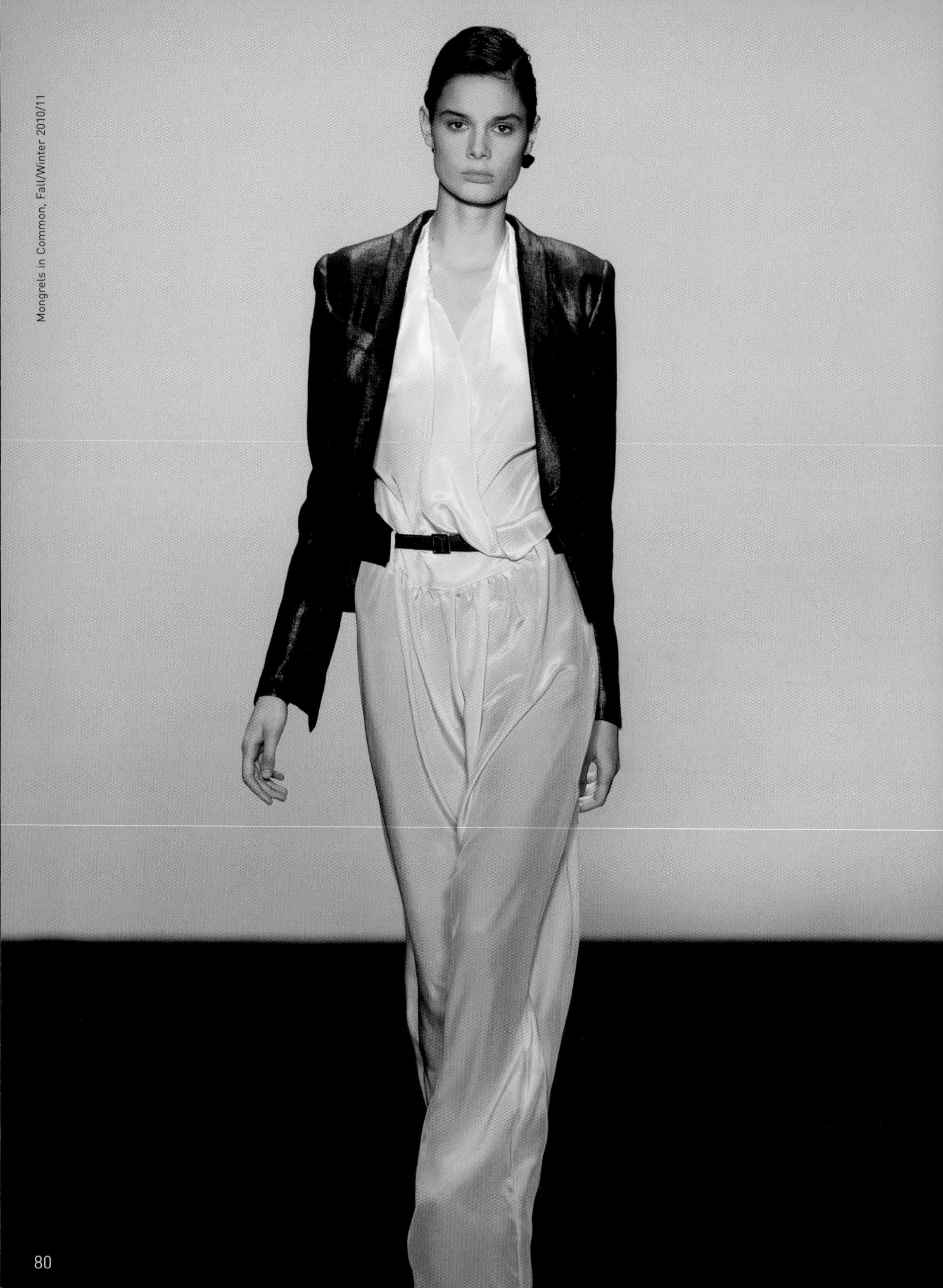

Mongrels in Common, Fall/Winter 2010/11

PATRICK MOHR

www.patrick-mohr.com

designer | Patrick Mohr

shop | Eastberlin
Alte Schönhauser Str. 33–34 | 10119 Berlin

INSIDER TIP : CULTURE

Sprüth Magers Gallery
www.spruethmagers.com
Oranienburger Str. 18 | 10178 Berlin

patrick mohr

Obwohl der Designer in München lebt, fühlt er sich sehr mit der Hauptstadt verbunden: „Die vielen Eindrücke, die ich auf den Straßen Berlins bekomme, sind für mich sehr inspirierend", sagt er. Als er im Sommer 2009 das erste Mal auf der Fashion Week zeigte, schickte er Obdachlose als Models über den Laufsteg. Eine seltsame Anmut strahlten sie aus: würdevoll und verstörend zugleich. Dasselbe könnte man auch über seine Kollektion sagen, mit der er mit althergebrachten Sehgewohnheiten bricht: Patrick Mohrs Kreationen liegen irgendwo zwischen Streetwear und Avantgarde, sind exzentrisch und haben immer einen Hang zur Provokation. Sicherlich nicht jedermanns Geschmack, aber dass er Talent hat, erkannten Profis sofort: 2007 verlieh ihm das Abschlussgremium der Münchner Modeschule ESMOD den „Prix Createur" für die beste Diplomkollektion seines Jahrgangs. Anschließend ging er ein halbes Jahr zum dänischen Designer Henrik Vibskov und gründete danach sein eigenes Label. Seit 2009 präsentiert er regelmäßig im weißen Zelt. „Als deutscher Designer möchte ich natürlich in meiner Heimat meine Mode zeigen."

Although he lives in Munich, designer Patrick Mohr feels very close to the capital. "The many impressions I get from its streets greatly inspire me," he says. In his first showing at Berlin Fashion Week in summer 2009 he sent a number of homeless people down the runway, who conveyed an odd sense of grace which at the same time was both wonderful and worrying. The same adjectives define his collection, with which he breaks all visual traditions. Patrick Mohr's eccentric creations are halfway between streetwear and avant-garde, and always with a touch of provocation. His fashion is probably not to everybody's taste, but his talent was immediately recognized by the fashion industry. In 2007 the jury of the ESMOD fashion school in Munich awarded him the Prix Createur for the best end-of-course collection. After six months working with the Danish designer Henrik Vibskov, he created his own label. Since 2009 his collections have been present in the White Tent at Fashion Week. "As a German designer, of course I prefer to show my work on home ground".

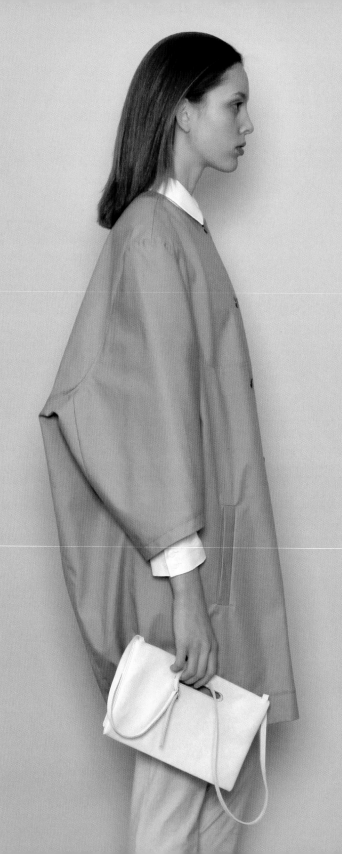

PERRET SCHAAD

www.perretschaad.com

designer | Johanna Perret, Tutia Schaad

shop | Ulf Haines Store
Rosa-Luxemburg-Str. 9 | 10178 Berlin

INSIDER TIP : CULTURE

Pro qm | www.pro-qm.de
Almstadtstr. 48–50 | 10119 Berlin

Im Januar 2010 wurden Johanna Perret und Tutia Schaad eingeladen, ihre erste Kollektion auf der Modewoche in Berlin zu zeigen. Im Sommer darauf folgte die zweite Präsentation. Daraufhin überschlug sich die Presse vor Begeisterung. „Ihre Modelle sind das Beste, was der deutschen Mode seit Jil Sander passiert ist", lobte später das SZ-Magazin. In der Tat erinnert ihr puristisch-eleganter Stil an den der großen deutschen Designerin. Perret Schaads Entwürfe sind bestechend schlicht, ohne dabei langweilig zu wirken. Dafür sorgen kleine Details, die aus einem einfachen Kleidungsstück etwas Besonderes machen. Trotz ihrer strengen Formsprache wirkt ihre Mode nie zu konstruiert, sondern hat immer etwas Weiches und Fließendes. Ihren Abschluss machten die beiden Designerinnen in Berlin an der Kunsthochschule Weißensee. Dort lernten sie sich kennen und gingen dann nach Paris, wo sie erste Erfahrungen bei Givenchy und Gaspard Yurkievich sammelten. Heute leben die gebürtige Münchnerin Johanna Perret und die aus Hanoi stammende Tutia Schaad wieder in der deutschen Hauptstadt, die sie inzwischen als „ihre Heimat" bezeichnen.

Johanna Perret and Tutia Schaad were invited to show their first collection at Berlin Fashion Week in January 2010. The following summer they took part with their second collection. The press was full of praise, "Their models are the best thing to happen to German fashion since Jil Sander", *SZ* magazine enthused. Indeed, their style, both classic and elegant, is reminiscent of Germany's fashion queen. Perret Schaad designs are captivatingly simple but never boring thanks to those small details that make a simple garment into something special. Although the basic lines are very strict, their clothes are never rigid and always includes a point of softness and suppleness. The two designers met while studying at the Weissensee School of Art in Berlin. They went to Paris together, where they acquired initial experience with Givenchy and Gaspard Yurkievich. Today, both Johanna Perret, originally from Munich, and Tutia Schaad, from Hanoi, are back in the German capital, which has become their 'homeland'.

Perret Schaad, Fall/Winter 2010/11

Perret Schaad, Spring/Summer 2011

Perret Schaad, Spring/Summer 2011

PRO QM

www.pro-qm.de

Almstadtstr. 48–50 | 10119 Berlin

PRO qm

Ein Inspirationsmekka für Kreative, Lesebegeisterte und Anhänger des Schönen bietet „Pro qm" in Mitte. Themenschwerpunkte des Sortiments sind die Stadt und ihre Schnittstellen zu Politik, Pop, Architektur, Design, Kunst und angrenzenden Theorien. Um das kulturelle Angebot abzurunden, organisiert „Pro qm" regelmäßig Veranstaltungen und Ausstellungen. Temporäre Buchhandlungen wurden hier unter anderem für den Frankfurter Kunstverein, das Kunsthaus Dresden und die Volksbühne in Berlin eingerichtet.

The Pro qm specialist bookstore in the Mitte district of Berlin is a paradise for creative types, book lovers, and art aficionados. It basically collects works on the city and its connections with politics, pop, architecture, design, art and other similar concepts. To round off the cultural offer, Pro qm organizes acts and exhibitions. Regular temporary book exhibitions for art and theater groups such as the Frankfurter Kunstverein, the Kunsthaus Dresden and the Volksbühne also take place here.

POTIPOTI

www.potipoti.com

designer | Silvia Salvador, Nando Cornejo

flagship store
Rosenthaler Str. 66 | 10119 Berlin

INSIDER TIP : CULTURE

Buchstabenmuseum
www.buchstabenmuseum.de
Karl-Liebknecht-Str. 13 | 10178 Berlin

Die beiden Spanier, die seit zehn Jahren in der deutschen Hauptstadt leben, sind eigentlich diplomierte Grafikdesigner. Kennengelernt haben sie sich an der Universität der Bildenden Künste in Salamanca. Danach gingen sie nach Madrid und arbeiteten dort als Art-Direktoren. 2001 zog es beide nach Berlin, wo sie ihrer Entwicklung freien Lauf lassen konnten. Diese mündete in der Gründung ihres eigenen Modelabels im Jahr 2005. Die Liebe zu ihrem Beruf sieht man ihren avantgardistischen Entwürfen an: In ihrer Kollektion spielen potipoti mit grafischen Elementen, die sich besonders in ihren abstrakten Mustern und Drucken zeigen – eine gelungen Synthese aus der Lebensfreude Spaniens und der rauen Urbanität Berlins. „Wir schöpften viel Inspiration aus der deutschen Hauptstadt mit ihrer Musik, den Menschen und der vielfältigen Clubszene", sagt das Designduo. Das städtische Berlin ist auch die Kulisse ihres Videoclips „Berlin Closer", in dem sie ihre Mode in spielerischen Collagen visuell in Szene setzen. Damit gewannen sie 2010 den ersten deutschen Fashion-Film-Award, der vom Bundesministerium für Wirtschaft und Technologie initiiert wurde.

These two Spanish artists, who are actually both graphic design graduates, have been living in the German capital for the past ten years. They met at the University of Fine Arts in Salamanca and later worked as art directors in Madrid before relocating to Berlin in 2001. Here they could give full rein to their professional capabilities, which led to the creation of their own label in 2005. The love for their profession is revealed in their razor-sharp designs: in their collection, Potipoti play with graphic details and apply them particularly to the abstract motifs and prints. In short, their work is a carefully balanced synthesis between the Spanish *joie de vivre* and a stark gray, urban Berlin. "The music, the people and the different nightspots of this city provide us with a great deal of inspiration," the designer duo says. Berlin itself is the backdrop to their video clip *Berlin Closer*, in which they visually embody their fashion through the use of animated collages. The short film won them first prize in last year's German Fashion Film Awards, an initiative of the Ministry of Economy and Technology.

BUCHSTABEN MUSEUM

www.buchstabenmuseum.de

Karl-Liebknecht-Str. 13 | 10178 Berlin

Die Liebe zur Typografie, Geschichte und zum Handwerk führt hierher. 2005 haben es sich Barbara Dechant und Anja Schulze zur Aufgabe gemacht, individuelle, handwerklich hochwertige Schriftzüge zu bewahren und diese einer breiten Öffentlichkeit zugänglich zu machen. So kann der Besucher heute eine außergewöhnliche Sammlung von Reklamen und typografischen Exponaten bewundern. Neben filigranen Buchstaben aus Bugholz zeigen sich dicke, schwere Edelstahlbuchstaben oder leuchtende Neonlettern. Die Designer von potipoti lassen sich hier zu neuen Entwürfen, Farbkombinationen und Drucken inspirieren.

The love of typography, history and artisan design led Barbara Dechant and Anja Schulze, in 2005, to consider amassing quality handmade examples of writing and displaying them to the general public. Today you can admire an exceptional collection of advertising signs and typographic works that feature different types of letters: heavy ones made from pure steel, dainty ones in solid wood, and neon signs. Here Potipoti's designers often find inspiration for their designs, color combinations, and prints.

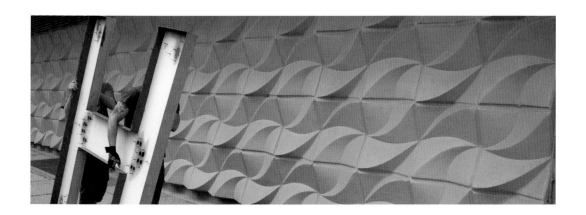

YTIJAƎЯ STUDIO

REALITY STUDIO

www.realitystudio.de

designer | Svenja Specht

shop | KONK
Kleine Hamburger Str. 15 | 10117 Berlin

INSIDER TIP : CULTURE

Kino International
www.kino-international.com
Karl-Marx-Allee 33 | 10178 Berlin

Alles begann mit einer rot-blauen Plüschjacke von Dior. Svenja Specht war fünf Jahre alt, als sie sie von ihrem Vater bekam. Sein Mitbringsel aus Paris sah völlig anders aus, als die Kleider, die sie hatte. Dieses extravagante Stück eröffnete ihr eine neue Realität. Noch immer beschäftigt sich die Designerin mit Bekleidung jenseits der Norm. So entwickelt sie zum Beispiel Modelle, die sich durch raffinierte Ärmelkonstruktionen, Ausschnitte oder Knopfdetails umfunktionieren und verändern lassen. Eines ihrer berühmtesten Teile ist ein Pullover mit vier Armen. Geboren in Neuss, studierte sie bis Ende der 1990er-Jahre Mode- und Produktdesign, ehe sie sich in die weite Welt begab. Nachdem sie in Peking und Paris genug Erfahrung gesammelt hatte, kam sie 2005 nach Berlin, um dort ihr Label zu gründen. „Paris und London sind zwar die großen Modemetropolen, aber nur schwer zu finanzieren", findet sie. In der Hauptstadt sei man hingegen offen, was neue Ideen betrifft. Ihr letztes Projekt ist eine Kooperation mit dem japanischen Sneaker-Profi Onitsuka Tiger. Zusammen mit ihm brachte sie im Frühjahr 2011 eine limitierte Schuhkollektion heraus. Im Winter 2011/12 wird eine weitere Sneaker-Kollaboration folgen.

It all began with a red and blue Dior plush jacket. Svenja Specht was five years old when her father brought it back from Paris for her. This extravagant item, completely unlike anything else in her wardrobe, opened up new horizons for her. Today the designer continues to create pieces that break established molds. For example, she creates multifunctional and transformable models using refined armholes, necklines, and button details. One of her best-known pieces is a four-sleeved jersey. Born in Neuss, she studied fashion and product design until the late 1990s, before setting off to work abroad. In 2005, after accumulating enough experience in Beijing and Paris, she moved to Berlin to found her own label. "It's true that London and Paris are the big fashion cities, but financially it's hard to get by there," she says. "Berlin, on the other hand, is open to new ideas." Her latest project has been in cooperation with the Japanese sneakers expert Onitsuka Tiger. Together they have launched into the market a limited footwear collection in spring 2011. This cooperation will be followed by another one based around sneakers for the 2011/2012 winter season.

Reality Studio, Spring/Summer 2010

Otsuka Tiger/Reality Studio Collaboration, Spring/Summer 2011

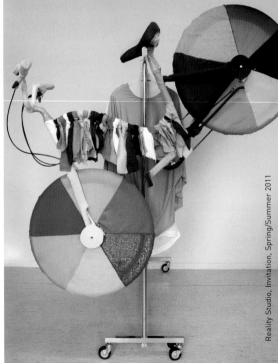

Reality Studio, Invitation, Spring/Summer 2011

Reality Studio, Spring/Summer 2010

Reality Studio, Fall/Winter 2010/11

KINO
INTERNATIONAL

www.kino-international.com | www.klub-international.com

Karl-Marx-Allee 33 | 10178 Berlin

Das ehemalige Vorzeige- und Premierenkino der DDR eröffnete bereits 1963 seine Pforten. Die Architekten Heinz Aust und Josef Kaiser schufen einen der gelungensten Kinosäle der Nachkriegszeit. Die denkmalgeschützte, bis heute original erhaltene glamouröse Ausstattung fasziniert die Besucher, die zu den zahlreichen im Haus stattfindenden Veranstaltungen wie Konferenzen, Messen, Konzerten, TV-Shows, Galadiners und Partys erscheinen. Neben dem gut ausgewählten Kinoprogramm findet in den ehemaligen Räumen der Bibliothek und dem Büro des Oktoberklubs einmal im Monat die Partyreihe „Klub International" statt.

The building of this former RDA cinema opened in 1963. Architects Heinz Aust and Josef Kaiser designed one of the most beautiful buildings of the post-war era. Its national heritage-listed decor, which still oozes its original glamour, is an object of fascination for everyone who attends the numerous events organized there: conferences, trade fairs, concerts, live television shows, banquets, and parties. Additionally, it puts on an excellent range of films once a month in the former library and the Oktoberklub office is the setting for the Klub International party.

SOPOPULAR

SOPOPULAR

www.sopopular.net

designer | Daniel Blechman

shop | F95
www.f95store.com

INSIDER TIP : CULTURE

Museum Hamburger Bahnhof
www.hamburgerbahnhof.de
Invalidenstr. 50–51 | 10557 Berlin

Daniel Blechman und den Brüdern James und David Ardinast blieb 2008 gar nichts anderes übrig, als SOPOPULAR zu gründen. In den letzten Jahren hatten die drei Kreativen – die früher Baggy Pants und Baseballcaps trugen und besessen von Sneakern waren – erfolglos nach einem Label gesucht, das die modischen Codes der Streetwear erwachsen umsetzt. Ebenso, dass auch über 30-Jährige wie sie sich damit identifizieren können, ohne wie Berufsjugendliche zu wirken. SOPOPULARs Zielgruppe sind heute jung gebliebene Männer, die mit beiden Beinen erfolgreich im Leben stehen. Ihre Kollektionen zeigen sich reduziert und pragmatisch. Klassische Schnitte und schmale Silhouetten werden mit kantigen Streetwearelementen gebrochen. Dafür sorgt der studierte Innenarchitekt Daniel Blechman, Designer und Kreativdirektor des Labels. Das Team legt großen Wert auf eine hochwertige Verarbeitung in Deutschland. SOPOPULAR distanzieren sich von der Schnelllebigkeit der aktuellen Modewelt und verfolgen das Ziel, moderne Klassiker mit Beständigkeit zu schaffen.

Daniel Blechman and the brothers James and David Ardinast had no choice but to found SOPOPULAR in 2008. For years the three artists, fans of baggy trousers, baseball caps and sneakers, had tried unsuccessfully to find a label which used the codes of streetwear fashion in an adult way. Their idea was for over 30-year-olds like themselves to be able to identify with these codes without appearing as adults masquerading as teenagers. SOPOPULAR's clothes clearly meet the criteria of the man who is young at heart but who has his feet on the ground. The collections could be described as reduced and pragmatic. Classic cuts and slim silhouettes are broken up with the most radical elements of streetwear, thanks to interior designer Daniel Blechman, the label's designer and creative director. The team attaches a great deal of importance to high-quality dressmaking, which is carried out in Germany itself. SOPOPULAR distances itself from the transient world of current fashion and pursues the goal of providing continuity to modern classics.

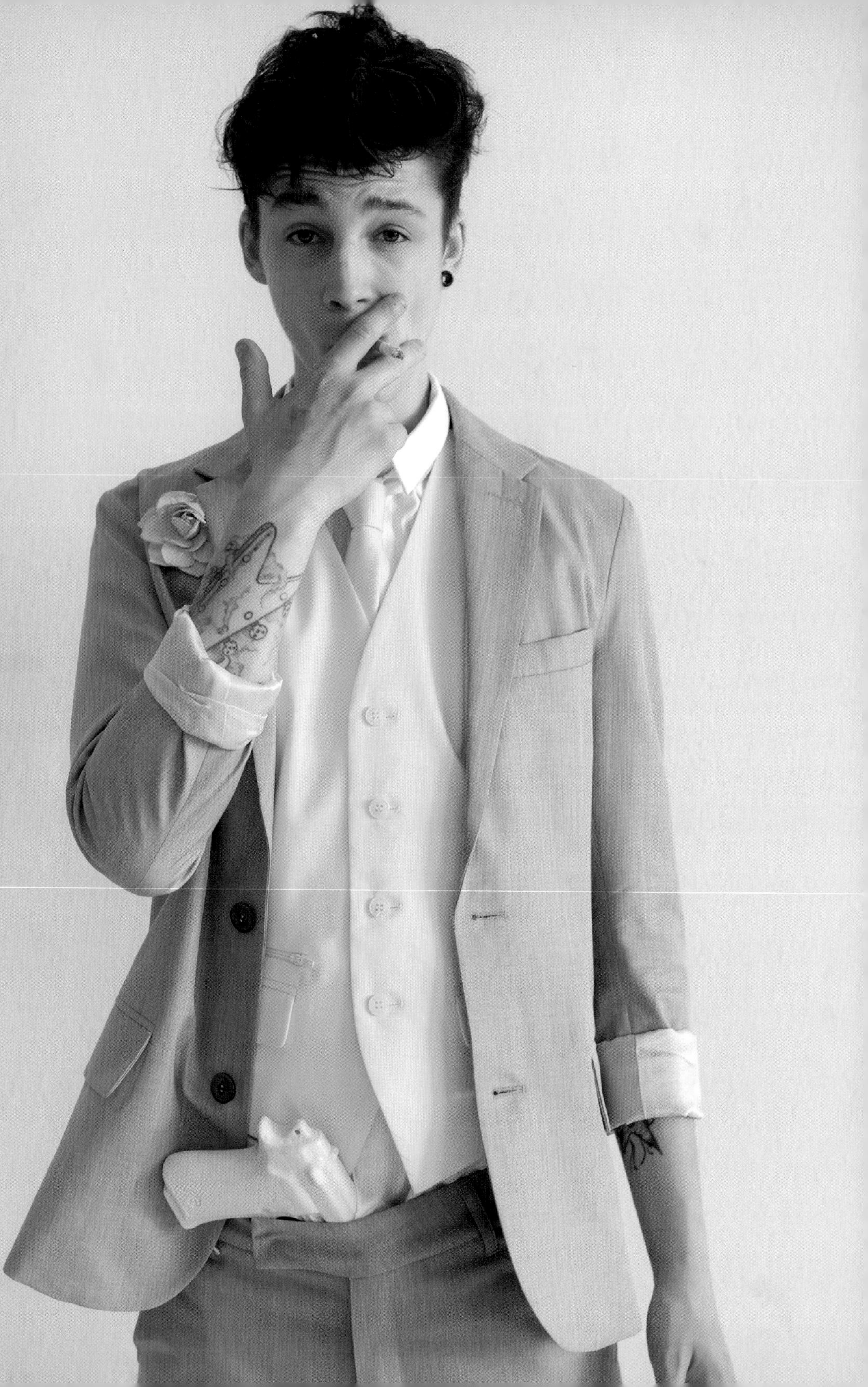

SOPOPULAR, Fall/Winter 2010/11

Starstyling, Fall/Winter 2010/11

STARSTYLING

www.starstyling.net

designer | Katja Schlegel, Kai Seifried

flagship store | Mulackstr. 4 | 10119 Berlin

INSIDER TIP : SHOPPING

Der Weiße Laden | Vintage
Mulackstr. 34 | 10119 Berlin

„Anti Avanti" versprühte im Sommer 2010 als eine der humorvollsten Präsentationen der Berlin Fashion Week richtig gute Laune. Die Designer von Starstyling spielen nicht nur mit Worten, sondern mit der Mode selbst. Denn Spaß steht für das Duo an erster Stelle! Dieser findet Ausdruck in explosiver Farbigkeit, verrückten Drucken, ungewöhnlichen Materialien, fantasievollem Schmuck und unerwarteten Kombinationen. Statt fertiger Looks bietet das Label modulare Mode und somit multifunktionale Stylingmöglichkeiten. Sein Klientel entscheidet selbst, welches Kleidungsstück es mit welchem Accessoire kombinieren will. Individualität wird großgeschrieben. So verwandelt sich ein schlichter Minirock je nach Lust und Laune durch Ankletten von bunten Stoffbahnen in einen luftig schwingenden Petticoat. Angefangen haben die studierte Kostümbildnerin und damals freie Stylistin Katja Schlegel und der Kommunikationsspezialist Kai Seifried 2000 mit ein paar handgefertigten Accessoires, die den beiden nur so aus den Händen gerissen wurden. Nach und nach erweiterten zuerst T-Shirts, dann immer mehr neue Kreationen das Angebot. Aus dem Hobby wurde ein spaßiger Hauptberuf.

Anti Avanti, one of the most entertaining shows at the Berlin Fashion Week in summer 2010 breathed a fine dose of good humor into the event. Starstyling's designers not only play with words but with fashion itself. For this pair, 'fun' is the top priority. This is embodied in the blast of colors, extravagant patterns, unusual materials, fantastic costume jewelry, and unexpected combinations. The brand distances itself from finished looks and offers versatile, multifunctional fashion. It is the customer who combines the clothing with the jewelry at will. Individualism is the name of the game. Depending on one's mood, a plain miniskirt can transform itself into a sheer, loose petticoat using pieces of multicolored fabric. Katja Schlegel, who trained as a wardrobe attendant and was a freelance stylist, and Kai Seifried, a communications specialist, started off in the year 2000 with a couple of handmade accessories that immediately flew off the shelves. They slowly expanded their offer, first with T-shirts and then with a whole array of new creations. The hobby has turned into a profession but it is still a pleasure.

LUXURY FASHION

INTRO

Berlin hat aufgeholt! In den letzten Jahren ist das Auftreten der deutschen Hauptstadt viel glamouröser geworden. Früher liefen die Trendsetter in Mitte mit Springerstiefeln und Parka durch Undergroundclubs, mittlerweile stöckelt die Szene durch angesagte Restaurants und Bars. Für solche Auftritte braucht man natürlich die passenden Kleider.

Die deutsche Avantgarde, die in Berlin sitzt oder hier auf der Fashion Week präsentiert, kommt diesem Bedürfnis nach. Sie wählt heute Berlin und nicht London oder Paris, um ihre Kollektionen zu zeigen. Mit der Fashion Week entstand hier eine internationale Plattform für deutsche Mode, die zu einem ständig steigenden Selbstbewusstsein der Szene sowie der Hauptstadt an sich beiträgt. Die Kollektionen der ehemaligen jungen, deutschen Wilden zeigen sich heute erwachsen. Ihre hochwertigen und extravaganten Modelle erregen Aufsehen. Klar, dass in den letzten Jahren eine ganze Reihe deutscher Labels, die mittlerweile für Qualität und Eleganz bekannt sind, internationale Erfolge verzeichnen konnte.

Dieses Kapitel präsentiert die Luxury-Designer Deutschlands, die tragbare Träume für Stars und Sternchen kreieren.

Berlin is now fashionably up to date! For years the city has been glamming up. While the trendy set used to attend Mitte's underground clubs in military boots and parkas, now they totter on heels among the coolest restaurants and bars. Of course they need a wardrobe to go with it.

The German fashion avant-garde, either established in Berlin or which presents at Fashion Week, satisfies these demands. Today it is Berlin rather than London or Paris where they prefer to show their collections. Berlin Fashion Week has created an international platform for German fashion, which is continually shoring up confidence in its fashion designers and in the city itself. The previously zany collections by young German designers have matured a great deal and their extravagant and quality models are making waves. This explains why recent years have seen a great many German labels achieve international renown for their quality and elegance.

In this chapter we present the luxury German designers dressing the stars of today and tomorrow.

DAWID TOMASZEWSKI

DAWID TOMASZEWSKI

www.dawid-tomaszewski.com

designer | Dawid Tomaszewski

showroom | Potsdamer Str. 97 | 10785 Berlin

INSIDER TIP | NIGHTLIFE

SOHO House | www.sohohouseberlin.com
Torstr. 1 | 10119 Berlin

Dawid Tomaszewski ist der neue Star am Berliner Modehimmel. Der gebürtige Danziger gründete sein Label 2009. Ein Jahr später feierte er im Sommer sein Fashion-Week-Debüt. Obwohl er bis dato noch völlig unbekannt war, konnte er bei der Modepresse punkten. Sogar die deutsche Vogue äußerte sich durchweg positiv über seine glamourösen Roben. „Ich möchte die Schönheit einer Frau unterstreichen und das Tragen meiner Kleider zu einem individuellen Erlebnis machen", sagt der Designer. Jedes seiner Modelle fertigt er per Hand, mit Nadel und Faden wie ein Couturier. Tomaszewski studierte zunächst Kunstgeschichte in Polen. Danach ging er nach London ans Royal College of Fashion. Anschließend zog es ihn nach Berlin an die Universität der Künste unter Vivienne Westwoods Leitung. Nach seiner Studienzeit widmete er sich zahlreichen Projekten, bevor er schließlich beim japanischen Modelabel Comme des Garçons als Assistent von Rei Kawakubo landete. Heute lebt Dawid Tomaszewski wieder in Berlin: „Die Kultur, meine Freunde und mein Team inspirieren mich jeden Tag aufs Neue, um diese Stadt mit Eleganz und Luxus zu erfüllen."

Dawid Tomaszewski is the new darling of Berlin fashion. Born in Danzig, Poland, he founded his label in 2009. A year later he debuted at the summer Fashion Week where he won over the fashion press, despite being an unknown. Even German Vogue praised his glamorous clothes. "My intention is to underline feminine beauty and ensure that wearing my clothes is a unique experience," the designer says. Like any good couturier, he personally finishes each of his models himself, needle and thread in hand. Tomaszewski started off studying Art history in Poland, before attending the Royal College of Fashion in London. He then went on to continue with his art studies at the University of Berlin, under the tutelage of Vivienne Westwood. Upon graduation, he turned to various projects before being taken on as an assistant to Rei Kawakubo at Japanese fashion label Comme des Garçons. Now he is living in Berlin again. "The culture, my people, and my team inspire new ideas in me every day that allow me to bring elegance and opulence to this city," he declares.

FRIDA WEYER

www.fridaweyer.com

designer | Frida Weyer

flagship store
Luckenwalder Str. 4–6 | 10963 Berlin

Frida Weyers Kollektionen erscheinen wie stoff-gewordene Träume. Die Designerin entwirft haupt-sächlich bezaubernde Cocktail - und Abendkleider aus fließenden Seidenmaterialien. Ihre Handschrift sind feminine und raffinierte Schnittführungen mit meist asymmetrischen und kunstvollen Drapie-rungen. Die auffälligen Kreationen werden gern von Celebritys auf den roten Teppichen dieser Welt getragen. Nach ihrem Abschluss an der interna-tionalen Modeschule ESMOD Berlin arbeitete die gebürtige Berlinerin in verschiedenen Bereichen der Modebranche, bevor sie im Januar 2009 letzt-endlich mit ihrer ersten eigenen Kollektion über-raschte. Prompt gewann Frida Weyer den „Premium Young Designers Award" und zeigte gleichzeitig als Finalistin des „Designer for Tomorrow Award by Peek & Cloppenburg" ihre Debütkollektion auf dem Catwalk der Mercedes-Benz Fashion Week. Seitdem präsentiert sie ihre Kollektionen zweimal jährlich im Rahmen der Modewoche an besonderen Orten – wie im Sommer 2009 – bei ihrer ersten Offside-Show im Chamäleon Vari-eté Theater. Kurz darauf wurde Frida Weyer mit Deutschlands renommiertestem Designaward, dem BUNTE „New Faces Award" ausgezeichnet.

Frida Weyer's collections are like dreams trans-formed into fabric. She mainly designs fasci-nating cocktail and evening dresses made from silky, sheer materials. Her hallmark is feminine and refined cuts, complemented with draped work that is generally asymmetrical and highly original. Celebrities offer to model her surpris-ing collections on the red carpet. After finishing her studies at the ESMOD international fashion school, this Berliner worked in different areas of fashion before surprising the world with her first own collection in January 2009. She was quickly given the Premium Young Designer Award and, at the same time, as a finalist in the Designer for Tomorrow Award by Peek & Cloppenburg, she presented her first collection on the run-way at the Mercedes-Benz Fashion Week. Since then her collections have been modeled twice a year at the Offside Show. The summer of 2007 was when she made her first appearance in the Chamäleon Varieté Theater. Not long after, Ger-many's Bunte magazine awarded her the presti-gious New Faces design award, one of the most renowned awards in German fashion.

Frida Weyer, Spring/Summer 2011

Frida Weyer, Spring/Summer 2011

CÔ CÔ

www.co-co.net

Rosenthaler Str. 2 | 10119 Berlin

Bánh mì nennt sich ein traditioneller Snack aus Vietnam. Bereits heiß begehrt in New York, London und Paris, ist er seit Oktober 2010 nun endlich auch in Berlin zu bekommen. Nach vietnamesischer Originalrezeptur wird das luftige Baguette aus Reismehl mit selbst gemachter Mayonnaise, asiatisch eingelegtem Gemüse, 24-Stunden mariniertem Fleisch oder Tofu, Koriander, Lauchzwiebeln und selbst gemachten Soßen nach Familienrezepten direkt vor den Augen der Besucher zubereitet. Das Gourmet-Deli Cô Cô bietet eine hervorragende Abwechslung zur bisherigen Snacklandschaft in Berlin-Mitte.

Báhn mì is the name of a typical Vietnamese sandwich. It was the talk of the town when it appeared in New York, London, and Paris and has been a hit at Berlin tables since October 2010. The sandwich, made to a traditional Vietnamese recipe, is prepared in front of the customer with soft bread made from rice flour. It is filled with homemade mayonnaise, marinated Asian vegetables, and meat that has been left to marinate for 24 hours, or tofu, cilantro, leeks, and a homemade sauce. The Gorumet-Deli Cô Cô offers this fantastic alternative to the regular array of sandwiches in Berlin Mitte.

HAUSACH
COUTURE

www.hausach-couture.com

designer | Sascha Gaugel

online shop | www.hausach-couture.com

INSIDER TIP : NIGHTLIFE

King Size Bar | www.kingsizebar.de
Friedrichstr. 112b | 10117 Berlin

Wie der Name schon sagt, bietet das Label Couture „nach französischem Maßstab", betont Sascha Gaugel. Diese entsteht aber nicht im schwarzwäldischen Hausach, sondern in Hamburg. Hausach ist lediglich Gaugels Hommage an den Geburtsort seiner Eltern. Bevor er in die Hansestadt zog, um 2006 sein Label zu gründen, machte der gebürtige Aachener seinen Abschluss in Düsseldorf an der Akademie für Mode und Design, kurz AMD. Seine aufwendigen Abendkleider zeigt er allerdings in Berlin. Ganz bewusst hat Sascha Gaugel die Metropole als seinen Präsentationsort gewählt: „Weil sie als Modestadt wachsen muss und alle Unterstützung brauchen kann, um international anerkannt zu werden", sagt er. Seinen ersten Beitrag leistete der Designer im Frühjahr 2010 auf der Fashion Week. Bei seiner Modenschau im weißen Zelt überraschte er das Publikum mit seinen fantasievollen Roben, die er meist aus italienischen Seidenstoffen fertigt. Seine Modelle mit den asymmetrischen Einsätzen, den ausladenden Drapierungen und den voluminösen Kragen überzeugten selbst die kritische Moderedaktion der Zeitschrift BUNTE. Zweimal schon zeichneten sie ihn dafür mit ihrem „New Faces Award" aus.

As the second part of the label's name suggests, "Couture designs follow in the lines of French patterns," says Sascha Gaugel. Despite the name, he did not found the label in the Black Forest town of Hausach, but in Hamburg. The name 'Hausach' was chosen simply to pay homage to where his parents were born. Before relocating to the hanseatic city of Hamburg to found his own label in 2006, the designer, born in Aachen, studied at the Academy for Fashion and Design (AMD) in Düsseldorf. Although resident in Hamburg, he intentionally shows his pricey eveningwear in the metropolis: "because Berlin has to grow as a fashion city and needs all the support it can get to become internationally renowned," he asserts. His first contribution to Fashion Week came in spring 2010, where the models in the White Tent stunned the public with fantasy-filled clothes usually created from Italian silk. His models with asymmetrical pieces, loose-fitting draping, and voluminous necklines even won over fashion magazine Bunte. He has won the New Faces Award twice.

Hausach Couture, Fall/Winter 2010/11

Hausach Couture, Spring/Summer 2009

Hausach Couture, Spring/Summer 2009

Hausach Couture, Spring/Summer 2009

kaviar gauche
berlin

KAVIAR GAUCHE

www.kaviargauche.com

designer | Johanna Kühl,
Alexandra Fischer-Roehler

flagship store | Linienstr. 44 | 10119 Berlin

INSIDER TIP NIGHTLIFE

CSA Bar | www.csa-bar.de
Karl-Marx-Allee 96 | 10243 Berlin

„Gauche kaviar" stand damals für den französischen Jetset, der gern mit den Ideen der 68er-Revolution kokettierte. Kaviar Gauche revolutionieren heute den Begriff Luxus mit ihrer konzeptionellen, femininen Avantgarde. Nach ihrem Abschluss an der Modeschule ESMOD in Berlin gründeten Alexandra Fischer-Roehler und Johanna Kühl 2004 ihr eigenes Label. Ihre erste Guerilla-Fashionshow vor dem Pariser Concept-Store „Colette" war der Startschuss einer internationalen Erfolgskarriere. Das Berliner Label zeichnet sich nicht durch Opulenz aus, sondern verleiht Luxus Tiefe, indem es ihn versteckt zum Ausdruck bringt – in exquisitem Material und innovativem Design. Grundintention bis heute ist die Symbiose von Accessoires und Kleidung. Taschenelemente werden auf Kleidung übertragen und typische Details von Kleidung auf das Taschendesign überführt. Inspiration schöpfen die Designerinnen auch aus der Natur. Typisches Merkmal sind immer wiederkehrende organische Elemente wie Lamellen, die sich auch bei der Einrichtung ihres neuen Flagship-Stores in Berlin-Mitte zeigen.

"Gauche-caviar" was the term coined for the French jet set that flirted with the ideas of the May 68 revolution. Today the conceptual and feminine avant-garde style of Kaviar Gauche is revolutionizing the notion of deluxe. After finishing their studies at the ESMOD international fashion school in Berlin, Alexandra Fischer-Roehler and Johanna Kühl founded their own label in 2004. Their first guerrilla marketing activity in front of the Colette department store in Paris launched their internationally successful career. This Berlin-based label is characterized, not by its opulence, but by the wealth of luxury indirectly highlighted through delicate materials and innovative designs. The main goal is to achieve a symbiosis between accessories and clothes: they apply details usually found in bags to clothes and vice versa. The designers find part of their inspiration in nature; they include a number of organic elements in both their garments and in the furniture in their new flagship store in the Mitte district of Berlin.

Kaviar Gauche, Spring/Summer 2011

Kaviar Gauche, Spring/Summer 2011

133

CSA BAR

www.csa-bar.de

Karl-Marx-Allee 96 | 10243 Berlin

ČSA®

Die Magazine Cosmopolitan und Wallpaper ernannten sie zum besten Mix aus Cocktail und Design in Ostberlin: Die CSA Bar, die 2001 im ehemaligen Gebäude der gleichnamigen tschechischen Fluggesellschaft eröffnete, erstrahlt heute in schönem 60er-Jahre-Design. Bei einem Ausblick auf den prächtigen Ostboulevard in Friedrichshain werden den Gästen erstklassige Cocktails serviert. „Die Karl-Marx-Allee ist typisch Berlin: großzügig, etwas grau und dennoch ergreifend. Die hell gehaltene und sehr stilvolle CSA Bar wirkt an diesem Ort völlig unerwartet. Ohne Hektik und Snobismus können wir hier klassische, gute Drinks in entspannter und geschmackvoller Atmosphäre genießen", so Kaviar Gauche.

The Cosmopolitan and Wallpaper magazines crowned it the best designer cocktail venue in East Berlin. The CSA Bar opened in 2001, in the old building of the eponymous Czech national airline. With views onto showy Ostboulevard in the hip Friedrichshain district, customers can enjoy an exquisite cocktail in a venue with a carefully designed 60s feel. "Karl Marx Avenue is typical of Berlin: generous, slightly gray, but nonetheless emotive. The CSA Bar is a place to savor good classic beverages at leisure in a calm, refined atmosphere," says the team at Kaviar Gauche.

KILIAN KERNER

www.kiliankerner.de

designer | Kilian Kerner

shop | BFN Concept Store
Rosenthaler Str. 40/41
Hakesche Höfe | Hof 3 | 10178 Berlin

INSIDER TIP SHOPPING

Achteinhalb | www.achteinhalb.com
Kollwitzstr. 42 | 10405 Berlin

Kilian Kerners Label lebt von Emotionen. Diese machen sich nicht nur in den innovativen Designs, den fließenden Stoffen in schmaler Silhouette, den Hosen mit tiefem Schritt, der Asymmetrie und dem Materialmix bemerkbar. Schon die Entscheidung, Mode zu seinem Beruf zu machen, wurde aus Kilian Kerners Leidenschaft für Kleidung und dem Gefühl geboren, dass das Designen in diesem Moment genau das Richtige für ihn war und ist. Zum Thema Ausbildung meint der Quereinsteiger, der sich früher als Schauspieler versuchte: „Ich habe mir mein Wissen durch Learning by Doing angeeignet und dieses in meinen ersten sechs Kollektionen stets erweitert." Inspirationen holt er sich aus seinem Inneren und Erlebten. Zu jeder Kollektion wird ein Lied komponiert, das ihr aktuelles Thema widerspiegelt. Im Sommer 2008 entschied sich Kilian Kerner, erstmals zur Modewoche zu zeigen. „Berlin ist mein Zuhause. Ich lebe und liebe hier. Die Mercedes-Benz Fashion Week in Berlin ist für mich immer die Taufe meiner Kinder", sagt der Designer ganz intuitiv.

The label Kilian Kerner is nourished on emotions, perceivable beyond the innovative designs: flowing materials on slim figures, low-slung pants, asymmetry and a combination of different fabrics. The decision to make fashion his profession arose from his passion for clothes and the intuition that told him that it was his vocation. In terms of education, the fashion designer, who didn't take the usual steps to becoming a fashion name and who had previously tried his hand at acting, says that his best school was 'learning through practice' and his first six collections. Kerner seeks inspiration within himself and his experiences. For each collection he writes a song, the theme of which reflects the concept. In summer 2008 Kilian Kerner decided to take part in Berlin Fashion Week for the first time. "This city is my home, it's where I live, and I love it." Mercedes-Benz Fashion Week Berlin is like the baptism of his 'babies', the designer says with complete naturalness.

Kilian Kerner, Fall/Winter 2010/11

Kilian Kerner, Fall/Winter 2010/11

Kilian Kerner, Spring/Summer 2010

ACHTEINHALB

www.achteinhalb.com

Kollwitzstr. 42 | 10405 Berlin

Im November 2010 wurde der angesagte Berliner Pop-Up-Store im Herzen vom Prenzlauer Berg sesshaft. Auf 80 m² vermischen sich Mode, Kunst und Musik – das lädt zum Inspirationsbesuch ein. Zwischen Kollektionen von außergewöhnlichen Berliner Designern wie Esther Perbandt, Clarissa Labin und Kilian Kerner präsentieren sich Schallplatten, Bücher und Bildbände über Fotografie, Kunst, Design und Architektur. Der Concept-Store dient hin und wieder als Plattform für Ausstellungen und Installationen junger Künstler. „ACHTEINHALB besticht durch ein tolles Sortiment und die nettesten Inhaber, die man sich vorstellen kann! Der Laden ist gemütlich und extrem charmant", so Kilian Kerner.

This reputable Berlin fashion store was established in the heart of Prenzlauer Berg in November 2010. Fashion, art, and music combine in the 860-square-foot space, inviting visitors to stay a while. The collections of extraordinary Berlin designers such as Esther Perbandt, Clarissa Labin, and Kilian Kerner, snuggle up here with records, books and a number of volumes on art, design and architecture. Every now and then the concept store is also used as a platform to showcase the exhibitions and installations of young artists. "ACHTEINHALB is impressive for its magnificent variety and for having the best owners you could hope for. The store is welcoming and elegant," Kilian Kerner declares.

KIMBERIT

www.kimberit.com

designer | Kim Berit Heppelmann

showroom
Reichenberger Str. 72a | 10999 Berlin

INSIDER TIP NIGHTLIFE

Club Wilde Renate | www.renate.cc
Alt-Stralau 70 | 10245 Berlin

Nach einer Schneiderlehre und einem Kostüm- und Modedesignstudium in Italien und den Niederlanden sammelte Kim Berit Heppelmann einige Erfahrung in verschiedenen Bereichen der Modebranche, bevor sie 2009 ihr eigenes Label gründete. Die Designerin versteht Mode als Kunstform und das Kleidermachen als Architektur der Bewegung. Ihre saisonunabhängigen Kollektionen sind tragbare Kunstwerke und scheinen ihrer eigenen Welt zu entspringen. Auf internationalen Fashion Awards wurde Kim Berit Heppelmann bereits mehrfach für ihre Haute-Couture-Kreationen ausgezeichnet. 2010 brachte sie zusätzlich die Ready-to-wear-Linie „Komment" auf den Markt. Sie ist ein Statement zu jeder neuen kimberit-Couture-Kollektion aus edelsten Materialien, bester Qualität und umgänglichen Preisen. Die Wahlberlinerin hat sich zum Ziel gesetzt, ökologische Mode aus einem hohen kreativen und künstlerischen Anspruch heraus zu entwerfen.

Following an apprenticeship as a designer and after studying fashion design in Italy and the Netherlands, Kim Berit Heppelmann worked in different sectors of fashion before creating her own label in 2009. For this designer, fashion is an artistic manifestation and the confection of architecture of movement. Her timeless collections are truly wearable works of art, whose origin spring from a different world. Kim Berit Heppelmann has received various international distinctions for her haute couture designs. In 2010 she also launched the ready-to-wear line Komment, which sums up the Kimberit model to a tee: models made using the finest materials and unbeatable quality at reasonable prices. This Berliner by adoption has set herself the goal of making environmentally friendly collections that are highly creative and full of fantasy.

KOSTAS MURKUDIS

KOSTAS MURKUDIS

www.kostasmurkudis.net

designer | Kostas Murkudis

shop | Potsdamer Str. 87 | 10785 Berlin

INSIDER TIP SHOPPING

Andreas Murkudis
www.andreasmurkudis.net
Potsdamer Str. 87 | 10785 Berlin

Kostas Murkudis kann man in vielerlei Hinsicht als Modepionier bezeichnen: 1994 gründete er in München sein Label und gewann noch im gleichen Jahr als einer der ersten deutschen Newcomer den damals wichtigen Philip-Morris-Award. Von 1996 bis 2001 präsentierte er seine Kollektionen zur Fashion Week in Paris, was ebenfalls ein Novum war. Zudem war er einer der Ersten, die unter ihrem Namen mit anderen Labels kooperierten, wie etwa 2004 mit dem Wäschehersteller Schiesser. Der Sohn griechischer Einwanderer studierte Modedesign an der Designfachschule Lette-Verein in Berlin. Nach einer Saison bei Wolfgang Joop ging er 1985 nach Wien zum österreichischen Avantgardedesigner Helmut Lang. Dort war er lange Jahre dessen rechte Hand, bis er sich schließlich selbstständig machte. Heute lebt und arbeitet er in Berlin, wo er im Sommer 2010 während der Modewoche sein Buch präsentierte. Darin dokumentiert Kostas Murkudis die Entstehung seiner Winterkollektion 2010, angefangen mit der Konzeption bis hin zur Produktion. Das Buch trägt den Titel „Luca" als Reminiszenz an das Model Luca Gadjus, seine Muse und Ideengeberin.

In many ways Kostas Murkudis can be considered a fashion pioneer. He founded his own label in Munich in 1994 and that same year took home first prize in the Philip Morris Awards which were highly prestigious at the time. He presented his collections in all the Paris Fashion Weeks between 1996 and 2001, again something of a novelty. What's more, he was one of the first designers to collaborate with other labels; for example, with the lingerie maker Schiesser in 2004. The son of Greek immigrants, he studied fashion design at the Lette-Verein School of Design in Berlin. In 1985, after a season working with Wolfgang Joop, he moved to Vienna to collaborate with Austrian avant-garde designer Helmut Lang. After being his right-hand man for many years, he finally decided to branch out on his own. Today he lives and works in Berlin. Here he presented his book during the summer of the 2010 Fashion Week, in which he documents the development of his winter 2010 collection from conception to production. The book is entitled *Luca*, in homage to the model Luca Gadjus, his muse and inspiration.

Kostas Murkudis, „Luca", Fall/Winter 2010/11

ANDREAS MURKUDIS

www.andreasmurkudis.net

Potsdamer Str. 87 | 10785 Berlin

ANDREAS MURKUDIS

Seit 2003 hat sich Andreas Murkudis ein kleines Imperium der schönen Besonderheiten inmitten Berlins aufgebaut. Der neue Laden in der Potsdamer Straße präsentiert die Welt von Andreas Murkudis, reich an Damen- und Herrenbekleidung, Designobjekten, Gepäck, Accessoires, Möbeln und allem, was das Kunst- und Modeherz sonst noch begehrt. Beim Inspirationsstreifzug durch die galerieartigen neuen Räume entdeckt man viele besondere Dinge, die in sonst keinem anderen Concept-Store zu finden sind. Wahrscheinlich ist Kostas Murkudis genau deshalb ein großer Fan vom Laden seines Bruders. Dass seine Kollektionen hier auch erhältlich sind, ist auf jeden Fall ein schöner Nebeneffekt.

Andreas Murkudis has run a little paradise for lovers of small treasures in the heart of Berlin since 2003. His new store on Potsdamer Strasse illustrates his world: a great variety of men's and women's clothing, design objects, items for travelers, accessories, furniture, and everything else that art and fashion connoisseurs could dream of. A wander through the new rooms, designed in the form of galleries, reveals many objects that cannot be found in any other concept store. No doubt that is why Kostas Murkudis is a permanent fixture in his brother's store. The icing on the cake is that his collections can also be found here.

LALA BERLIN

www.lalaberlin.com

designer | Leyla Piedayesh

flagship store | Mulackstr. 7 | 10119 Berlin

INSIDER TIP NIGHTLIFE

The Broken Hearts Club
www.thebrokenheartsclubberlin.com
Choriner Str. 44 | 10435 Berlin

„Gut ist nur gut, was sich gut anfühlt", hat Leila Piedayesh einmal gesagt. Und das trifft auch auf ihre Mode zu. Ihre lässigen Entwürfe aus Strick sind nicht nur schick, sondern auch äußerst bequem. Um dieses Gefühl zu erreichen, verwendet sie nur feine Materialien: Kaschmir, Seide, edle Baumwollgarne und Jersey. Bevor Leila Piedayesh 2003 mit ihrem Label durchstartete, studierte sie BWL und war Redakteurin bei dem Musik- und Lifestylesender MTV. Die Designerin hat immer schon gern gestrickt, und weil ihre ersten Entwürfe reißenden Absatz im Freundeskreis gefunden hatten, kam sie auf die Idee, es mit einem eigenen Label zu versuchen. Piedayesh fing zunächst mit dem Entwerfen von Tüchern an und benannte ihr Label nach ihrem Spitznamen Lala. „Und nach Berlin, der Stadt, die ich liebe", erklärt sie. Ein Jahr später zeigte sie ihre Pali-Tücher aus Kaschmir bereits auf der Modemesse Premium Exhibitions und traf damit den Nerv der Zeit. Heute begeistert Lala Berlin mit einer kompletten Kollektion selbst Hollywoodstars wie Mischa Barton, Cameron Diaz und Jessica Alba.

"Good things are only good if they are nice to touch," Leila Piedayesh once said. This philosophy is perfectly applicable to her fashion. Her relaxed knitwear creations are not just pretty but also extraordinarily comfortable. To achieve this sensation she uses exquisite materials: cashmere, silk, premium cotton, and jersey. Before Leyla Piedayesh embraced her design sensibility by launching her own line in 2003, she studied business administration and was an editor for MTV. She has always liked to knit and, after seeing how popular her designers were among her acquaintances, decided to create her own label. She started off she designing scarves under the label Lala Berlin —Lala being her nickname "and Berlin, for the city I love". A year later she showed her Arabic cashmere headdresses at the Premium Exhibitions fashion fair, all having been adapted to the spirit of the times. Nowadays Lala Berlin and her collections have become very popular with certain Hollywood actresses including Mischa Barton, Cameron Diaz, and Jessica Alba.

LaLaBerlin, Spring/Summer 2010

LaLaBerlin, Spring/Summer 2011

Marcel Ostertag, Fall/Winter 2010/11

MARCEL OSTERTAG

www.marcelostertag.com

designer | Marcel Ostertag

online shop | www.8pieces.com

Marcel Ostertag

INSIDER TIP : FOOD
Grill Royal | www.grillroyal.com
Friedrichstr. 105 b | 10117 Berlin

Mode aus London ist innovativ, progressiv, inspi-rierend und irgendwie immer anders. Mit seinen Kollektionen, die genau dieses Flair versprühen, rüttelt Marcel Ostertag, der seinen Abschluss am renommierten Central Saint Martins College in London absolvierte, heute die deutsche Modeszene wach. Der Avantgardedesigner, dessen Atelier und Showroom sich in München befinden, blickt über den „deutschen Tellerrand" hinaus. Er präsentierte seine Kollektion sogar schon auf der Modewoche in Peking. Inzwischen ist Marcel Ostertag fester Bestandteil der Mercedes-Benz Fashion Week: „Ich bin Deutscher, und natürlich bietet Berlin als Hauptstadt die beste Möglichkeit, meine Kollek-tionen zu präsentieren." Seine Modenschauen sind bis auf die letzten Plätze besetzt, weisen stets eine hohe Promidichte auf und sorgen für ein großes Presseecho. Die Exklusivität Ostertags glamouröser Kollektionen, die eine Hommage an den Ladylook der späten 1970er- und 1980er-Jahre sind, belohnten bereits diverse Preise wie der Moët & Chandon-Fashion-Award.

London fashion is innovative, progressive, in-spiring, and somehow always different. With his collections steeped in these concepts, Marcel Ostertag, a former student of the celebrated University of Arts/Central Saint Martins College London, is revolutionizing the German fashion scene. This razor-sharp designer, whose ate-lier and showroom are in Munich, crosses na-tional borders with his creations. He has even presented his collections at the Beijing Fashion Week. He has become a regular at Mercedes-Benz Fashion Week: "I am German, so of course Berlin as a capital offers me the best possibili-ties for presenting my collections". His runway shows are usually packed and attended by nu-merous celebrities. They also are assured press coverage. The exclusive and glamorous collec-tions with which he pays homage to the femi-nine looks of the 1970s and 1980s, have won him various prizes, including the Moët & Chandon Fashion Award.

Marcel Ostertag. Fall/Winter 2010/11

GRILL ROYAL

www.grillroyal.com

Friedrichstr. 105 b | 10117 Berlin

GRILL
ROYAL

Aus riesigen Schaukühlschränken wählt hier der Gast hervorragendes Fleisch aus tiergerechter Haltung und frischen, exzellenten Fisch selbst aus. In angenehmer Atmosphäre gestaltet es sich relativ leicht, vor dem alten Speedboot, das auch James Bond in den 1960er-Jahren gehört haben könnte, gemütlich bei einem Glas Champagner auf die feinen Speisen aus der offenen Küche zu warten. Ein Grill mal ganz anders – königlich eben. „Mein Insidertipp ist das Grill Royal, weil das Essen dort gut ist und man die interessantesten Leute trifft", so Marcel Ostertag.

It is the diner who chooses organic meat or an excellent fresh fish from a giant glass fridge. It is agreeable to linger over a delicious glass of champagne while your exquisite meal is being prepared in the open kitchen of this former vessel that looks like something out of a 1960s James Bond film. It is a splendidly unique steak restaurant. "My personal recommendation is the Grill Royal, because of its great food and you can meet with the most interesting people," Marcel Ostertag says.

MICHALSKY

www.michalsky.com

designer | Michael Michalsky

flagship store
Potsdamer Platz 4 | 10785 Berlin

MICHALSKY

┌──┐
│ INSIDER TIP ┊ NIGHTLIFE   │
│ **Asphalt Club** | www.asphalt-berlin.com │
│ Mohrenstr. 30 | 10117 Berlin   │
└──┘

„Real Clothes For Real People" lautet die Designphilosophie von Michael Michalsky. Wie man tragbare Kleidung für moderne Menschen kreiert, versteht er. Und auch, wie man sie glamourös in Szene setzt: Seine StyleNite, auf der er während der Berliner Fashion Week seine Mode inszeniert, dauert die ganze Nacht und gehört mittlerweile zum Pflichtprogramm für sämtliche Stylisten und Moderedakteure. Der gebürtige Göttinger weiß eben, wie man sich gut verkauft. Kein Wunder, bei seinem Lebenslauf: Bevor er 2006 sein Label gründete, war er über zehn Jahre für Adidas tätig. 2000 stieg er zum internationalen Kreativdirektor auf und entwickelte zusammen mit Yohji Yamamoto die exklusive Linie Y-3. Nach wie vor arbeitet er für viele andere Marken wie Sony, Audi, BMW und Afri Cola. Neuerdings entwirft er auch für das Sportswearlabel Kappa, das zu einem chinesischen Sportartikelkonzern gehört. Seine eigene Kollektion ist ebenfalls sehr sportlich geprägt, gemischt mit klassischen und luxuriösen Elementen. Man sieht es ihr an, dass er sehr von Berlin beeinflusst ist. „Diese Stadt bietet einfach unendlich viel Inspiration", sagt er. Deshalb hat Michalsky dort auch seinen Firmensitz.

Michael Michalsky's designs are based on the mantra 'Real Clothes For Real People'. Nobody else knows how to create such wearable fashion for modern people and at the same time present it with such élan: StyleNite, in which he presents his collections at Berlin Fashion Week, runs through the night and has become a must for stylists and fashion journalists. The Göttingen-born creator knows how to sell himself. Not surprising, given his professional background: before setting up his label in 2006 he worked at Adidas for more than 10 years. In 2000 he was appointed creative director and together with Yohji Yamamoto developed the exclusive Y-3 line. As in his previous career, he also works for other labels, including Sony, Audi, BMW, and Afri Cola. Nowadays he also designs for the sportswear label Kappa, part of a Chinese sporting goods consortium. His own collection, also very sports-oriented and which combines classic and luxury elements, shows the influence of Berlin. "This city is highly inspiring," he says. That is why Michalsky is headquartered in the German capital.

Michalsky, Spring/Summer 2011

Michalsky, Spring/Summer 2011

ASPHALT CLUB

www.asphalt-berlin.com

Mohrenstr. 30 | 10117 Berlin

ASPHALT

Gepflegt feiern lässt es sich im angesagten Asphalt Club in den Tiefen des Hilton Hotels am Gendarmenmarkt in Berlin-Mitte. Die Symbiose aus Restaurant, Bar und Club ist der neue Treffpunkt der Berliner Avantgarde- und Partyszene. Das puristische Ambiente verdankt der Club dem Büro „karhard", den Architekten des bekannten Clubs Berghain. Die internationale Küche, die leckeren Cocktails und das weltklasse DJ-Line-up laden zu einem genussvollen Abend bis in die Morgenstunden ein. Mode trifft auf Musik, wenn verschiedene Modelabels wie Michalsky mit Live-acts wie Aloe Blacc oder DJ Hell ihre Partys feiern.

Parties are made to be enjoyed at the Asphalt Club on the first floor of the Hilton Hotel on Gendarmenmarkt in the Mitte district of Berlin. The symbiosis of restaurant, bar and club makes it a new meeting place and event venue for the Berlin avant-garde. The classic style comes from the Karhard studio, also the architects of the famous Berghain club. The international cuisine, delicious cocktails, and exceptional DJs promise an unforgettable night that can last well into the early hours. Fashion fuses with music when designers like Michalsky hold events there with artists such as Aloe Blacc and DJ Hell.

Penkov, Spring/Summer 2011

PENKOV

www.penkovberlin.com

designer | Bernadett Penkov

shop | Departmentstore | Quartier 206
Friedrichstr. 71 | 10117 Berlin

INSIDER TIP : SHOPPING

Flohmarkt am Mauerpark
www.mauerparkmarkt.de
Bernauer Str. 63–64 | 10435 Berlin

In ihrer Mode verbindet Bernadett Penkov Gegensätze miteinander: Feminines mit Maskulinem, Romantik mit Strenge und Leichtigkeit mit Funktionalität. „Die Frau, die Penkov trägt, soll sich stark und unbeschwert fühlen", so lautet ihr Ziel. Mit ihren präzisen Entwürfen hat Bernadett Penkov es längst erreicht. Schon zweimal gewann sie den Moët & Chandon-Fashion-Award: einmal 2005 mit dem Label „MaisonAnti", zusammen mit ihrer damaligen Geschäftspartnerin, das zweite Mal 2006 mit ihrer eigenen Kollektion, die sie ein Jahr zuvor ins Leben rief. 2008 zeigte sie erstmals auf der Berlin Fashion Week. Ein Jahr später wurde sie als einziges deutsches Label von der EU eingeladen, um Deutschland auf der Tokioter Modewoche zu repräsentieren, obwohl die Designerin ursprünglich Ungarin ist. Geboren in Budapest, kam sie bereits im Kindesalter nach Deutschland und wuchs in Nordrhein-Westfalen auf. Dort studierte sie zunächst BWL und Psychologie. 1999 beschloss Bernadett Penkov, nach Berlin zu ziehen, um Design an der Modeschule ESMOD zu studieren. „Diese Stadt finde ich spannend und neu", verrät sie. In Anbetracht ihres Erfolgs war dies sicherlich ein guter Schritt.

Bernadett Penkov's fashion plays with contrasts: feminine and masculine, romanticism and rigidity, lightness and functionality. "The woman who wears Penkov should feel strong and worry-free," is her motto. Thanks to her precise creations, Bernardett reached her goal some time ago. She has now won the Moët & Chandon Fashion Award twice: once in 2005 with the label MaisonAnti, together with her former partner, and again in 2006, with a collection of her own that she had created the year before. She took part in Berlin Fashion Week for the first time in 2008 and a year later was selected and invited by the European Union to represent German fashion at Tokyo Fashion Week, despite her Hungarian background. Born in Budapest, her family moved to North Rhine-Westphalia when she was small. There she studied business administration and psychology. She moved to Berlin in 1999 to study design at the ESMOD fashion school. "This city is exciting and new," she comments. Given the success of her designs she undoubtedly made the right decision.

Penkov, Spring/Summer 2011

Penkov, Spring/Summer 2010

Penkov, Spring/Summer 2011

Penkov, Spring/Summer 2011

Penkov, Spring/Summer 2010

Sabrina Dehoff, Spring/Summer 2011

ACCESSORIES

Julia Menthel, Fall/Winter 2008/09

INTRO

Was wäre die Mode ohne ihre Accessoires? Erst sie runden ein Outfit perfekt ab oder unterstreichen einen Stil. Dieses Kapitel in CITY FASHION BERLIN ist eine kleine Exkursion in das interessanteste Taschen-, Schuh- und Schmuckdesign, welches sich in der Modemetropole Berlin sammelt. Die deutschen Accessoiresdesigner sind bekannt für ihre überlegten, oft detailverliebten Entwürfe. Sie wollen keine großen Kollektionen in Masse produzieren wie die vielen bekannten Marken, die neben ihrer Mode mittlerweile von Taschen bis hin zu Schuhen allen möglichen Schnickschnack entwerfen, um den Umsatz noch weiter anzukurbeln. Im Gegensatz dazu haben sich die in diesem Kapitel gezeigten Designer ausschließlich auf das Kreieren von modischem Beiwerk spezialisiert und überzeugen mit ihren individuellen Designs. Sie legen Wert auf Handwerk und grenzen sich mit ihren innovativen Kollektionen von der breiten Masse ab. In einer kreativen Stadt wie Berlin finden ihre experimentellen Kollektionen Anerkennung.

Where would fashion be without accessories? Firstly they set off an outfit or highlight a style. This chapter of CITY FASHION BERLIN proposes an exciting foray into the design of the most interesting bags, shoes, and jewelry on the Berlin fashion scene. German accessories designers are known for their carefully designed models which reflect their love of detail. Unlike many well-known labels which design bags, shoes, and other accessories in addition to clothes in order to boost sales, the designers in this chapter turn their backs on mass production. Specializing exclusively in the creation of fashion accessories with a highly convincing style, they attach a great deal of importance to the quality of the manufacturing, and thanks to the originality of their collections distance themselves from the mass. In a creative city like Berlin their collections enjoy well-deserved fame.

ANJA BRUHN

anja bruhn

www.anja-bruhn.com

designer | Anja Bruhn

shop | BFN Concept Store
Rosenthaler Str. 40/41
Hackesche Höfe | Hof 3 | 10178 Berlin

INSIDER TIP : SHOPPING
Kompliment Showroom
Jablonskistr. 20 | 10405 Berlin

Bereits während ihres Modedesignstudiums an der Hochschule FHTW entwarf Anja Bruhn Taschen für das Berliner Label Kaviar Gauche. Wie das geht, wusste sie bereits, denn das Handwerk hatte sie bei einem Schneider gelernt. Ihre Leidenschaft für Accessoires brachte sie 2006 auch in ihrer Abschlussarbeit mit ein. Nachdem sie ihr Diplom buchstäblich in der Tasche hatte, gründete die Designerin ein Jahr später ihr eigenes Label. Neben Handtaschen entwirft sie heute Clutches, It-Bags, Portemonnaies, Laptoptaschen und Gürtel. Besonders markant sind ihre Modelle mit Metallic-Beschichtungen. Anja Bruhn steht für luxuriöses Design. Logisch, dass sie dafür nur edle Materialien verwendet: Lammnappa, Kalbsleder oder Ziegenleder. Im Juli 2009 präsentierte sie ihre Taschen erstmals auf der Fashion Week. Gemeinsam mit Modemacher Kilian Kerner entwickelte sie die Accessoirelinie Kerner & Bruhn und zeigte sie auf seiner Show im Zelt am Bebelplatz. „Berlin ist eine kreative Metropole. Durch die Fashion Week hat sie sich als Modehauptstadt in ganz Deutschland etabliert", sagt die gebürtige Berlinerin. „Da liegt es nahe, dass auch ich hier meine Entwürfe präsentiere."

While studying fashion design at the FHTW School of Fashion Design, Anja Bruhn created handbags for Berlin label Kaviar Gauche, a skill she had acquired when working as a tailor and dressmaker. In 2006 she reflected her passion for accessories in her end-of-course work. Diploma in hand, she decided to set up her own label the following year. As well as handbags, she currently designs clutch bags, 'it' bags, purses, laptop bags, and belts. Of particular note are the models coated in leather foils. Anja Bruhn relishes high-end design so it is no surprise that she uses only quality materials, such as lamb nappa leather, calfskin, and goatskin. Her bags made their Fashion Week debut in July 2009. Together with clothes designer Kilian Kerner, she developed the accessories line Kerner & Bruhn and presented it in a fashion parade of the designer in the marquee on Bebelplatz square. "Berlin is a creative metropolis which, thanks to Fashion Week, has established itself as the fashion capital of the whole of Germany. So it stands to reason that I also present my creations here," this native Berliner states.

FIONA BENNETT

www.fionabennett.com

designer | Fiona Bennett

flagship store
Alte Schönhauser Str. 35 | 10119 Berlin

INSIDER TIP : NIGHTLIFE

Kosmetiksalon Babette
www.barbabette.com
Karl-Marx-Allee 36 | 10178 Berlin

Ein Hut bringt ein Gesicht erst richtig zur Geltung. Fiona Bennett hat es sich zur Aufgabe gemacht, dafür einen Rahmen zu schaffen. Geboren in Brighton, kam sie bereits als Kind mit ihren Eltern nach Westberlin. Dass sie einmal Hutmacherin werden wollte, wusste sie damals schon: „Das war immer mein geheimer Wunsch", erzählt sie. 1988 absolvierte Fiona Bennett ihre Ausbildung zur Modistin. Gleich im Anschluss daran machte sie sich selbstständig und entwickelte einen eigenen Stil. Dieser zeigt sich romantisch verspielt mit einem Hauch Nostalgie und geht oft mit ironischem Schabernack einher: Auf manchen ihrer Hüte landen Vögel, oder es wachsen Früchte darauf. Fiona Bennetts Kreationen sind Haute Couture für den Kopf. Mehr für den Alltag geeignet ist ihre Zweitlinie „Kiss by Fiona Bennett", die sie 2009 einführte. Diese Hüte und Mützen, hauptsächlich aus Alpakawolle, sind für die kalte Jahreszeit gedacht. Die Designerin genießt ihr Leben in Berlin. Ob sie jemals in ihre Heimat zurückkehren würde? Warum sollte sie? „In Berlin kann man gut in Ruhe arbeiten", findet die Britin.

A hat can highlight a face and Fiona Bennett has made it her main aim to do just that. Although she was born in Brighton in the UK, her family moved to West Berlin when she was very young. Even then she knew that one day she would work as a milliner. "It was always my secret desire," she confesses. In 1988 Fiona Bennett finished her milliner's course, became a freelance designer, and developed her own romantic and slightly wistful style. She is often daring with creations that have a certain touch of irony: it is not unusual to see hats sporting birds' nests or bearing fruit. Fiona Bennett creations are haute couture for the head. For daily wear there is her second line, Kiss by Fiona Bennett, which she created in 2009. These hats and caps, generally in alpaca wool, are designed for the cold seasons. The designer enjoys living in Berlin. Would she like to go back to Britain? "Why" she asks, "when you can work calmly in Berlin?"

FIONA BENNETT

KOSMETIKSALON BABETTE

www.barbabette.com

Karl-Marx-Allee 36 | 10178 Berlin

Ursprünglich sollte der Glaspavillon, der schon 1962 fertiggestellt wurde, Ende der 1980er-Jahre neben dem sowjetischen Nationalitätenrestaurant Café Moskau als Ausstellungs- und Verkaufsraum für Kunstgewerbe der UdSSR dienen. Seit der feierlichen Eröffnung des Gesamtensembles 1965 mit dem Kino International, dem Café Moskau, der Mokka-Milch-Eisbar und den weiteren Wohn- und Geschäftsgebäuden auf der Karl-Marx-Allee befindet sich die Bar Babette – zu DDR-Zeiten ein Kosmetiksalon – im Originalzustand.

The glass pavilion was finished in 1962 and, together with the restaurant Nationalitätenrestaurant Café Moskau, it was used as a showroom and sales point for designers from the USSR until the end of the 1980s. Bar Babette is located on Karl Marx Avenue, within the complex that comprises Kino International, Café Moskau, the Mokka Milch Eisbar, and various other commercial and residential buildings. The bar, which in Communist times was a cosmetics salon, opened its doors in 1965 after a solemn inauguration of the complex. Its original state has been preserved.

JULIA MENTHEL

www.agencyv.com/julia-menthel

designer | Julia Menthel

shop | Andreas Murkudis
Potsdamer Str. 87 | 10785 Berlin

INSIDER TIP : SHOPPING
Voo Store Berlin | www.vooberlin.com
Oranienstr. 24 | 10999 Berlin

Julia Menthel ist bekannt für ihre feinmaschigen Ketten aus Edelstahl, die sich elegant um den Hals oder ums Handgelenk schmiegen. Sie wirken wie ein metallener Stoff, dessen Optik die Designerin mit Bändern, Garnen oder japanischen Akoya-Perlen bricht. Ihre glänzenden Netze, in Silber und Gold, verarbeitet sie auch in ihren Ohrringen. Eine weitere Besonderheit sind die auffälligen Haarreifen mit Federn. Die Berlinerin studierte zunächst Modedesign in Florenz und New York, wo sie ihren Bachelor am Fashion Institute of Technology absolvierte. Hier arbeitete sie dann als Accessoiredesignerin bei dem Modelabel Anne Klein. Anschließend wechselte sie als kreative Beraterin in die Schmuckabteilungen von Calvin Klein und Tommy Hilfiger. Bei ihnen entdeckte sie ihre wahre Liebe für das edle Geschmeide. Über London, wo Julia Menthel am Central Saint Martins College of Art einen einjährigen Designkurs belegte, kehrte sie nach Berlin zurück. Dort gründete Julia Menthel 2006 ihre eigene Schmucklinie mit dem Ziel, zeitlose Klassiker zu entwerfen.

Julia Menthel is known for her fine mesh stainless-steel chains that adapt to the neck or wrist. The designer softens the metal look by winding ribbons, threads, or Japanese akoya pearls into the pieces. Her shiny gold and silver chains can also be turned into earrings. Other specialties include extravagant feathered diadems. This Berliner studied fashion design in Florence and New York, where she graduated from the Fashion Institute of Technology. She worked as an accessories designer for fashion label Anne Klein in New York before going on to freelance as a jewelry design consultant for Calvin Klein and Tommy Hilfiger. This is where she discovered her true love for high-end jewelry. Following a one-year stint in London, where she enrolled on a design course at the University of Arts/Central Saint Martins College London, Julia returned to Berlin, and set up her own jewelry and costume jewelry line in 2006. Her ambition is to create timeless classics in jewelry that never goes out of fashion.

VOO STORE BERLIN

www.vooberlin.com

Oranienstr. 24 | 10999 Berlin

Der Concept Fashion Store versteckt sich in einem Hinterhof, völlig untypisch und bisher auch einzigartig – nämlich in Kreuzberg. Neben internationalen Modemarken von Streetwear bis hin zu topmodernen, bekannten Kollektionen verbergen sich hier schöne Kleinigkeiten aus den Bereichen Kunst und Design. Unter Büchern, Kerzen und Parfüms findet man in der ehemaligen Schlosserei sicherlich ein neues Lieblingsstück zum Mit-nach-Hause-Nehmen. Der Voo Store Berlin versteht sich außerdem als Plattform für Musik, Design und Mode und organisiert deswegen regelmäßig Ausstellungen, Installationen und Konzerte internationaler Künstler.

This concept store is hidden in a rear courtyard, a somewhat unusual place for this type of establishment, at least for the Kreuzberg neighborhood. Among international streetwear labels and well-known collections of the latest fashion, you can find small works of art and design objects. With so many books, candles, and perfumes, it is almost impossible to leave this former locksmith's empty-handed. Voo Store Berlin is also committed to the latest in music, design and fashion. It regularly holds exhibitions, art installations, and concerts by internationally renowned artists.

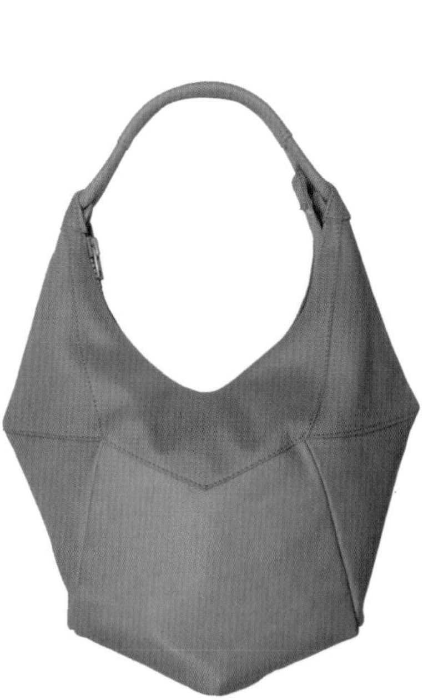
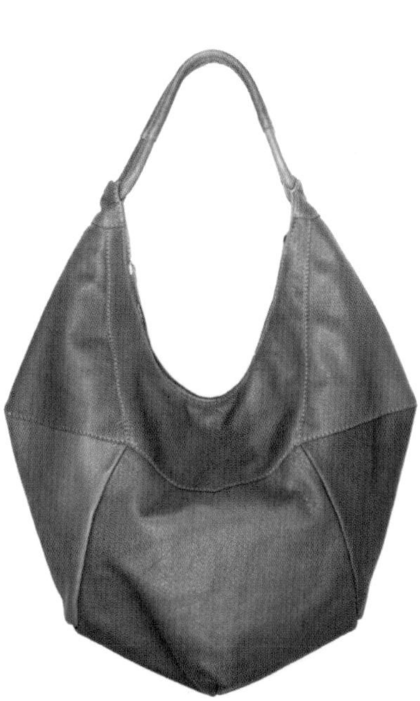
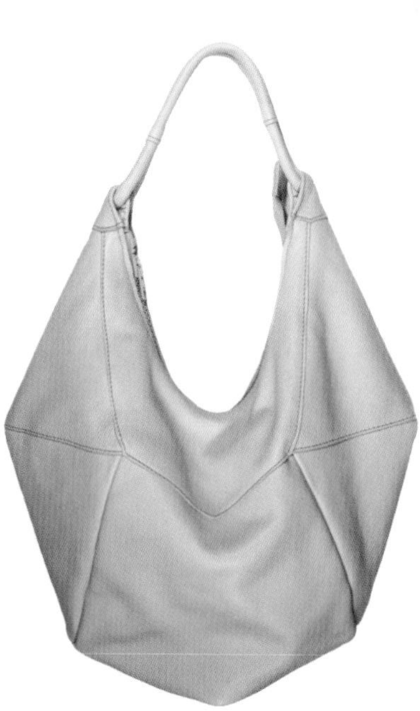
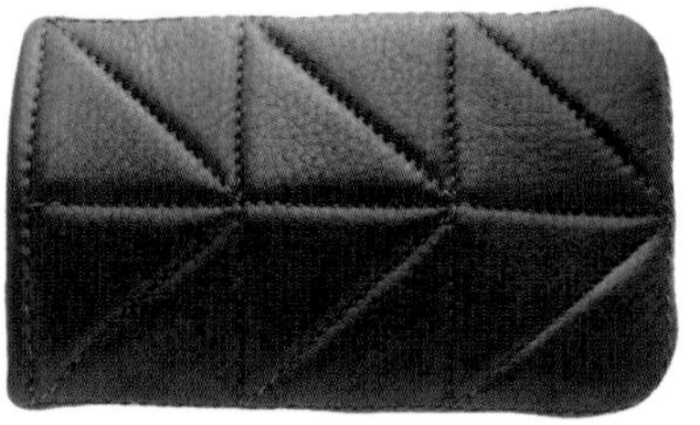
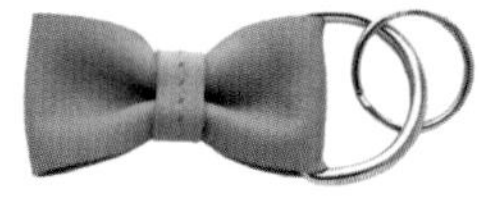
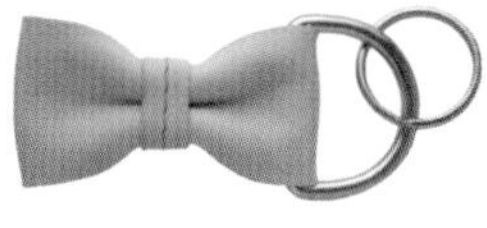
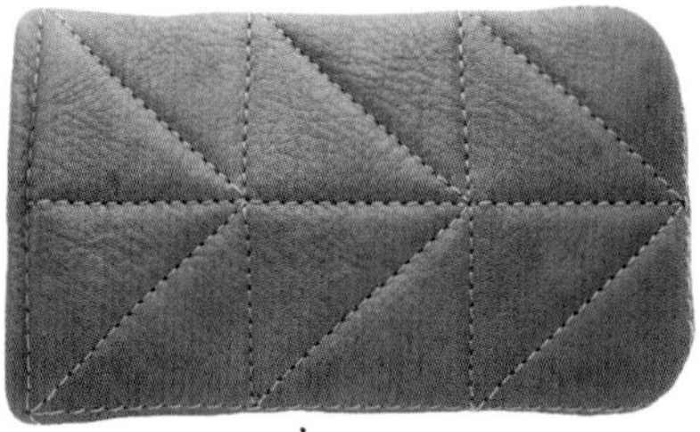
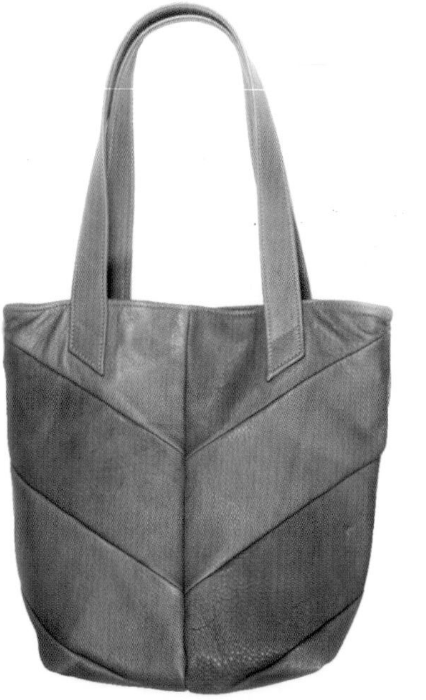
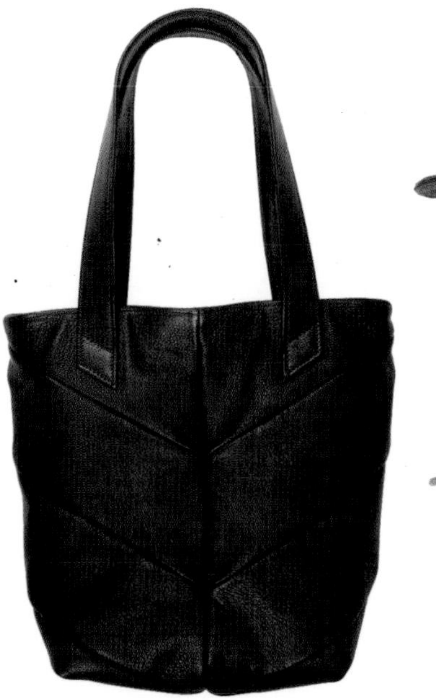
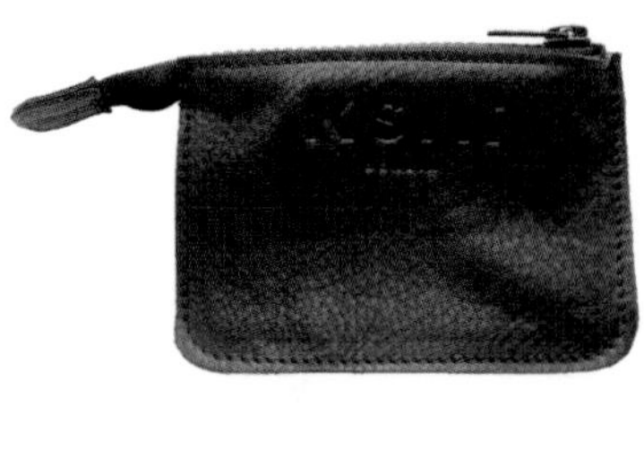
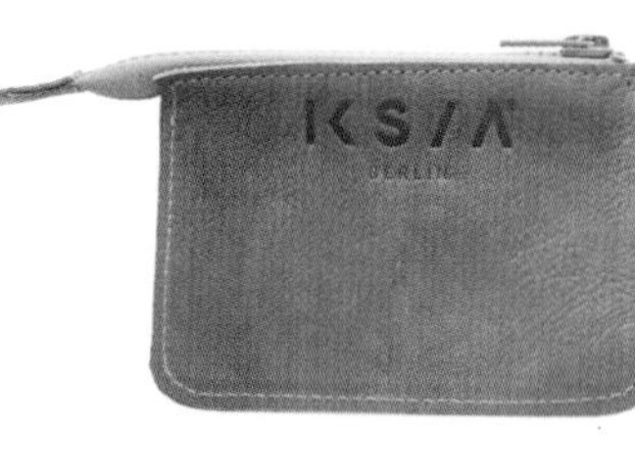

KSIA, Spring/Summer 2011 + Fall/Winter 2010/11

KSIA

www.ksia-berlin.de

designer | Kasia Ehrhardt

shop | ecoShowroom
Almstadtstr. 35 | 10119 Berlin

INSIDER TIP SHOPPING

ecoShowroom | www.ecoshowroom.de
Almstadtstr. 35 | 10119 Berlin

Aus dem Ökotrend ist eine Lifestylebewegung geworden, die die ehemals unvereinbaren Aspekte Öko und Modernität auch in der Mode miteinander verbindet. Die Architektin und Modedesignerin Kasia Ehrhardt entwirft Taschen, die umwelt- und sozialverträglich in Deutschland entstanden sind und dabei trotzdem gut aussehen. 2010 gründete sie ihr Ökolabel KSIA. Die Accessoirekollektion besteht ausschließlich aus pflanzlich gegerbtem Rindsnappaleder, das sich durch eine extreme Geschmeidigkeit bei hoher Widerstandsfähigkeit auszeichnet. Alle Lederaccessoires werden in Handarbeit in Berlin hergestellt. Wie eine geradlinige und gut durchdachte moderne Architektur zeichnen sich auch die Handtaschen durch eine geometrische Schnittführung und klare Linien aus. So ließ sich Kasia Ehrhardt für ihre Sommerkollektion 2011 von der richtungsweisenden Berliner Nachkriegsarchitektur der 1950er- und 1960er-Jahre inspirieren. Die Accessoires kommen, wie die Architektur, ohne überflüssige Dekoration aus. Puristisch und klar sind auch die Farben, die Kasia Ehrhardt mit ihrem Wissen über das Kolorit der Berliner Nachkriegsarchitektur bewusst gewählt hat.

The eco-friendly trend is the origin of a movement that blends aspects previously considered irreconcilable even within the world of fashion, such as ecology and modernity. The lovely bags that architect and designer Kasia Ehrhardt makes are produced in Germany, and while taking solidarity and the environment into consideration the beauty of her bags is not compromised. In 2010 she founded the line KSIA. The organically tanned cow leather, from which she makes all the accessories in the collection, is noted for its softness and resistance. All the leather accessories are artisan-made in Berlin. Exemplifying a straight-lined, modern, and thoughtfully considered architecture, her bags are characterized by their geometrical cuts and clear lines. For her summer 2011 collection, Kasia Ehrhardt has drawn on post-war Berlin architecture from the 1950s and 1960s. The accessories, offer a simple, flourish-free design. Kasia took great care in choosing the light, pure colors reminiscent of post-war Berlin, something she could do because of her profound knowledge of the city.

ecoSHOWROOM

www.ecoshowroom.de

Almstadtstr. 35 | 10119 Berlin

Berlin-Mittes erster grüner Concept-Store, der sonst nur temporär zu den Modewochen existierte, öffnete im November 2010 endlich ganzjährig seine Pforten. Der ecoShowroom bietet eine breite Palette an ausgesuchten Produkten traditioneller, aber auch noch unbekannter biologischer Firmen. Neben Mode internationaler Ökomarken wie KSIA und Vilde Svaner präsentiert der ecoShowroom auch Kosmetik, Lebensmittel und Wohnartikel – alles rein ökologisch.

The first environmentally friendly concept store in mid-town Berlin, which used to open only temporarily during the Fashion Week periods, is open all year round now since November 2010. EcoShowroom boasts of a wide range of traditional products and little-known environmentally friendly brands. As well as fashion by internationally renowned organic labels such as KSIA and Vilde Spaner, it also stocks cosmetics and food products, as well as household items —all of which are eco-friendly.

MYKITA

MYKITA

www.mykita.com

designer | Philip Haffmans, Daniel Haffmans, Harald Gottschling, Moritz Krüger

MYKITA Shop Berlin
Rosa-Luxemburg-Str. 6 | 10178 Berlin

INSIDER TIP FOOD

Papà Pane | www.papàpane.com
Ackerstr. 23 | 10115 Berlin

Spätestens seit „Sex and the City" kennt Franz jeder. Franz? Das ist ein Brillenmodell von Mykita, das Carrie Bradshaw im zweiten Teil des Kinofilms trägt. Dass sie einmal auf Jessica Parkers Nase landen würde, hätten sich die vier Berliner nicht gedacht, als sie 2003 ihr Label gründeten. Damals war ihr Atelier noch in einer ehemaligen Kindertagesstätte, kurz „Kita", untergebracht. Aus dem englischen Wort „my" und „Kita" entstand dann der Labelname. Mykita setzt auf Handarbeit: Bei ihren Brillen sind Fassung und Bügel so geformt, dass man sie einfach zusammenstecken kann. Schrauben werden dadurch überflüssig. Alle Modelle, egal, ob klassisch-elegant oder avantgardistisch, werden in der eigenen Manufaktur in Berlin hergestellt. Keine andere Stadt käme für die vier Freunde infrage: „Im Gegensatz zu anderen Metropolen ist in der Hauptstadt der Begriff Etikette ein Fremdwort. Es gibt keine Benimmregeln oder Kreise, in die man erst aufgenommen werden muss. Das vermittelt den Menschen ein Gefühl von Zwanglosigkeit und bildet einen guten Nährboden, auf dem sich kreative Geister entfalten können."

If they weren't before, everyone is now familiar with the Franz model of Mykita eyewear since it turned up in the second part of *Sex and the City*, as worn by the character Carrie Bradshaw. The four Berliners who founded the label in 2003 could never have imagined their glasses would end up on Sarah Jessica Parker. At the time the studio was still located in a former children's nursery called Kita, to which they added the word "My" to make the label's name. The company works in an artisan fashion: the frames and earpieces are produced in a way that allows them to fit perfectly, doing away with the need for screws. All the models, whether classic, elegant, or avant-garde, are manufactured in their own factory in Berlin. The four friends have never considered changing city. "Unlike other metropolises, here no one wants to label you or put you into a box. You don't have to follow any rules or a particular hierarchy to be accepted. You feel free to create in a relaxed fashion, which makes this place a perfect milieu for creative minds," they say.

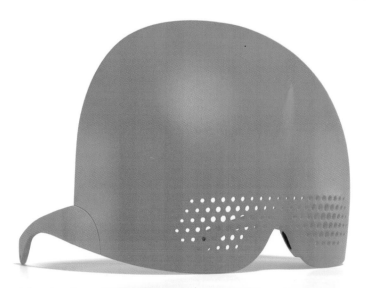

Top to bottom: MYKITA X Rad Hourani, Spring/Summer 2011, MYKITA X Bernhard Willhelm, Spring/Summer 2011, MYKITA X Romain Kremer, AW 2010

Top to bottom: MYKITA, Spring/Summer 2011, MYKITA X Alexandre Herchowitch, Spring/Summer 2011, MYKITA, Spring/Summer 2011

Rike Feustein, Spring/Summer 2009

RIKE
FEURSTEIN

www.rikefeurstein.com

designer | Rike Feurstein

flagship store
Rosa-Luxemburg-Str. 28 | 10178 Berlin

INSIDER TIP : FOOD

Chipps | www.chipps.eu
Jägerstr. 35 | 10117 Berlin

„Ein Hut sollte nicht nur irgendein Kopfschmuck sein, sondern mit der Person, die ihn trägt, harmonieren", sagt die Modistin. Rike Feurstein ist der Magie von Hüten verfallen. Dafür gab sie sogar ihre Karriere als Rechtsanwältin auf und erlernte das Handwerk von Grund auf in traditionellen Couture-Werkstätten in London und New York. Danach zog es die gebürtige Freiburgerin nach Berlin, wo sie 2006 ihr Label gründete. Ihre skulpturhaften dreidimensionalen Modelle sind wahre Hingucker. Sie erinnern an Hüte aus den 1940er- und 1960er-Jahren, die sie heute modern interpretiert. „Das Besondere an meinen Kreationen sind ihr Minimalismus und ihre Klarheit", verrät sie und lüftet damit ihr Geheimnis. Ihre Kopfbedeckungen fertigt Rike Feurstein in ihrem Berliner Atelier per Hand. Dafür verwendet sie nur natürliche Materialien wie Wolle, reine Seide, Panamastroh, Kaninchenhaarfilz und Nappaleder. Im Sommer 2008 präsentierte das Label seine Kreationen in Kooperation mit „JOOP! Jeans" zum ersten Mal auf der Berlin Fashion Week.

"A hat should never be just an accessory to adorn a head, but should be in keeping with the person who wears it," this designer says. Rike Feurstein was so fascinated by the magic of hats that she gave up her law degree and began to learn her current trade in the traditional dressmaking studios of London and New York. This German designer from Freiberg later relocated to Berlin, where she founded her own label in 2006. Her three-dimensional sculptural models are true works of art. They resemble the hats of the 1940s and 1960s but with a modern twist. "The thing about my creations is their minimalist lines and clarity," she says, revealing her secret. Rike Feurstein makes her models in an artisan tradition in her Berlin atelier, using only natural materials such as wool, silk, Panama straw, angora, and nappa leather. The label presented its creations at the Berlin Fashion Week for the first time in summer 2008, in cooperation with JOOP! Jeans.

Rike Feurstein for Joop! Jeans, Spring/Summer 2008

Rike Feurstein for Joop! Jeans, Spring/Summer 2008

Rike Feurstein, Collage, 2009

CHIPPS

www.chipps.eu

Jägerstr. 35 | 10117 Berlin

Chipps bietet seinen Gästen frische, leichte Küche und wechselnde, saisonal angepasste Gerichte. Bei Sonnenschein kann man das Ganze auf der Terrasse genießen. Ob zum gemütlichen Frühstück, zum schnellen Lunch oder zum gemeinsamen Dinner – im Chipps kommt jeder auf seine Kosten. Das Restaurant ist gleichermaßen für Vegetarier und Fleischesser konzipiert. Bei einem Essen in gemütlicher Atmosphäre und ansprechendem, schlichtem Design können die Feinschmecker dem Koch in der offenen Küche über die Schulter schauen.

Chipps offers customers a cuisine of fresh, light market produce in dishes that change according to the season. Weather permitting they can be enjoyed on the terrace. Whether it is a delicious breakfast, a quick lunch, or dinner with friends you are after, at Chipps you will find a dish to suit your pocket. The restaurant serves vegetarian cuisine and delicious meat meals. The welcoming, simply designed establishment affords diners the chance to see their meals being prepared in the open-plan kitchen.

Sabrina Dehoff, Spring/Summer 2011

SABRINA DEHOFF

SABRINA DEHOFF

www.sabrinadehoff.com

designer | Sabrina Dehoff-Helmbold

flagship store | Torstr. 175 | 10119 Berlin

INSIDER TIP : CULTURE

Neues Museum | www.neues-museum.de
Bodestr. 1 | 10178 Berlin

Nach ihrem Modedesignstudium an dem Aus-bildungszentrum Lette-Verein in Berlin verschlug es Sabrina Dehoff-Helmbold nach London, wo sie das Royal College of Art besuchte, um ihren Master zu absolvieren. Danach war sie in Paris als Womenswear-Designerin für die Modehäu-ser Guy Laroche und Lanvin tätig. Letztendlich kehrte Dehoff-Helmbold 2000 mit einer Menge Erfahrung und noch mehr Ideen für die Zukunft wieder nach Berlin zurück. Sie gründete die Desig-nagentur vonRot und war hier als Beraterin für internationale Modemarken tätig. Seit 2006 widmet sie sich ganz ihrer Leidenschaft, dem Schmuck-design. Ihre Anhänger, die an langen feingelied-rigen Ketten hängen, erscheinen luftig leicht wie die Federn, die daran flattern. Ihre Entwürfe hatten früher immer etwas Verspieltes, wirken heute aber abstrakter und puristischer. Mittler-weile hat die Designerin ihr Sortiment erweitert und fertigt nun auch Armbänder aus Textilkordeln in meist kräftigen Farben an. Laut dem „World Luxury Guide" zählt Sabrina Dehoff-Helmbold zu den zehn interessantesten Schmuckdesigner-innen der Welt. Nebenbei ist die engagierte Krea-tive seit 2007 Partnerin und Geschäftsführerin der Presse Agentur „Agency V" in Berlin.

After studying fashion design at the Lette-Ver-ein School of Design in Berlin, Sabrina Dehoff-Helmbold relocated to London to do a Master's degree at the Royal College of Art. She then moved to Paris to work as a designer on the womenswear lines of the fashion labels Guy Laroche and Lanvin. Dehoff-Helmbold finally returned to Berlin in 2000 with a wealth of ex-perience and bursting with ideas for her future projects. First she founded the fashion consul-tancy company vonRot and worked as a consul-tant for various international fashion labels. She has devoted herself to her passion, jewelry de-sign, since 2006. Her pendants, suspended from long, fine necklaces, appear as lightweight as the feathers they contain. At first her creations always had a playful quality about them, but now they have evolved into purer and more abstract lines. The designer has also expanded her range to include textile cord bracelets, nearly always in bright colors. The *World Luxury Guide* lists Sabri-na Dehoff-Helmbold as one of the top 10 most promising jewelry designers in the world. This committed creator has also been a partner and the general manager of the Berlin-based press group Agency V since 2007.

Top to bottom: Boss, Fall/Winter 2009. Slingshot, Spring/Summer 2000. Rope (Prototype), Spring/Summer 1999. Dream, Fall/Winter 2010. Rectangle, Fall/Winter 2009.

trippen

TRIPPEN

www.trippen.com

designer | Angela Spieth, Michael Oehler

flagship store | Rosenthaler Str. 40/41
Hackesche Höfe 4 + 6 | 10178 Berlin

INSIDER TIP : CULTURE

Radialsystem V | www.radialsystem.de
Holzmarktstr. 33 | 10243 Berlin

Die Schuhe von Trippen sind ein Berliner Original. 1994 gegründet, ist es eines der ältesten und erfolgreichsten Labels aus der Post-Wende-Zeit. Lange bevor der Begriff Nachhaltigkeit in Mode kam, hatten ihre Gründer bereits den Anspruch, modernes Design langlebig und umweltfreundlich zu gestalten. Mit Erfolg: Mittlerweile ist Trippen auf der ganzen Welt mit Partnershops vertreten. Allein in Berlin gibt es drei eigene Stores. Die beiden Macher stammen aus Süddeutschland und kamen noch vor dem Mauerfall nach Westberlin. Während Angela Spieth an der Hochschule der Künste, heute UdK, Modedesign studierte, machte Michael Oehler seinen Schuhmachermeister. Die perfekte Ergänzung also, um sich gemeinsam kreativ zu entfalten. „Berlin bietet dafür genau den notwendigen Freiraum", sagen sie. Bis heute ist das Designduo auf der Suche nach dem „perfekten Schuh", obwohl sie ihn längst gefunden haben. Ihre Modelle bestechen durch ihr außergewöhnliches Design, das oft an Schuhe aus dem Mittelalter erinnert. Selbst der japanische Designer Issey Miyake ist davon angetan. Mit ihm begann 2003 eine langjährige Kooperation.

Trippen shoes are Berlin originals. The label, founded in 1994, is one of the oldest and most successful to be created during the time of German reunification. Before the concept of sustainability became fashionable, its founders had already proposed creating a long-lasting, modern design that would respect the environment. This goal has become a success story and Trippen footwear can now be found the world over, but only in Berlin do Angela Spieth and Michael Oehler have three stores of their own. The pair, originally from southern Germany, came to Berlin after the fall of the wall. While Angela Spieth studied fashion design at the Berlin State School of Fine Arts (today the Berlin University of the Arts), Michael Oehler trained as a shoemaker. They therefore formed a perfect couple to develop their creativity together. "Berlin offers all the space needed for it," they say. The designers continue to seek 'the perfect shoe', although many people say they have already found it. Their models are popular because of their original designs and they are somewhat reminiscent of shoes from medieval times. They began a longstanding cooperation with Japanese designer Issey Miyake, a big Trippen fan, in 2003.

RADIALSYSTEM V

www.radialsystem.de

Holzmarktstr. 33 | 10243 Berlin

Hier tanzt die Musik! Das RADIALSYSTEM V hat sich seit seiner Gründung 2006 als offener Raum für den Dialog der Künste etabliert. Der historische Name des transformierten Pumpwerks am Spreeufer ist Programm: Das RADIALSYSTEM V bringt Künstler, Kreative und Kulturbegeisterte in Kontakt miteinander und entwickelt aus der Begegnung von Tradition und Innovation, Alter Musik und zeitgenössischem Tanz, bildender Kunst und Neuen Medien neue Genres: von choreografischen Konzerten und Opern über Nachtmusik im Liegen, Barock-Lounge, Konzertinstallationen bis hin zu Familientagen.

The place where the music itself dances! Since its creation in 2006, RADIALSYSTEM V has been an open venue for different artistic expressions. The former pumping station on the banks of the River Spree honors its name: RADIALSYSTEM V brings together artists, creators, and culture vultures to develop unusual genres formed from the contact between tradition and innovation, early music and modern dance, visual arts and new media forms. It puts on choreographies and operas as well as the Nachtmusik series in which the audience listens to Barock-Lounge (billed as 'where baroque meets electro') while lying peacefully on yoga mats. It even hosts family celebrations.

Zeha, Fall/Winter 2010/11

ZEHA

www.zeha-berlin.de

designer | Alexander Barré, Torsten Heine

flagship store
Kurfürstendamm 188-189 | 10707 Berlin

INSIDER TIP : SHOPPING

F95 Store | www.f95store.com

zeha berlin

Eigentlich wollten Alexander Barré und Torsten Heine lediglich den Turnschuh ihrer Jugend wieder auf die Straße bringen. 2003 beschlossen sie, eine kleine Edition nur für Bekannte anzufertigen, doch aufgrund der großen Begeisterung blieb es nicht dabei. Also riefen sie die 1897 von Carl Häßner in Thüringen gegründete Schuhfirma Zeha, die 1960 offizieller Ausstatter der DDR-Olympiamannschaft war, wieder ins Leben. Das Ergebnis sind heute straßentaugliche Sneaker in Anlehnung an die legendären Originalmodelle im modernen Retrostil. Seit 2006 vereint das neue Symbol als Dachmarke die drei Kollektionen Streetwear, Carl Häßner und Urban Classics. Die Kombination aus Wort- und Bildmarke zeigt die Siegessäule Viktoria als Berliner Wahrzeichen mit einem typischen Zeha-Schuh in ihrer Hand. Das Symbol steht hierbei für Berlin und zeigt die Verbindung von Alt und Neu, von Tradition und Moderne. „Berlin ist Schmelztiegel verschiedener kultureller Einflüsse, die uns inspirieren. Berlin hat eine ganz eigene unorthodoxe Art, mit Mode umzugehen und Trends zu interpretieren. Wir nehmen diese Trends auf und setzen sie in unserem eigenen Zeha Berlin typischen Design um", so das Kreativteam.

Alexander Barré and Torsten Heine's original idea was to bring the sports shoes of their youth back into fashion. In 2003 they created a limited edition just for friends and acquaintances but it was so successful they took the idea further. In 2003, they began to remanufacture the Zeha footwear label that had been founded by Carl Häßner in Thuringia in 1897 and which in 1960 produced the official sport shoes for the German Democratic Republic's Olympic team. The outcome is streetwear sneakers that borrow the legendary retro style of the original model. This new symbol has been bringing the Streetwear, Carl Häßner, and Urban Classics collections together since 2006. The label's logo is the Victory Column as a symbol of Berlin, with Victoria holding aloft a Zeha shoe. It is a representation of the city that shows the conjunction of old and new, tradition and modernity. "Berlin is a melting pot of different cultural influences that inspire us. It has its own and highly original way of considering fashion and interpreting its trends. We capture them and turn them into our own Zeha Berlin design," the pair say.

Zeha, Fall/Winter 2010/11

F95 STORE

www.f95store.com

Ein Muss für Trendsetter und Modeinteressierte ist der F95 Store. Das Shoppingmekka der Macher der großen Modemesse Premium, die zweimal jährlich in Berlin stattfindet, steht den Pilgern ganzjährig offen. Der F95 Store bietet nicht nur ein gut gemischtes Sortiment aus modernen Jeansmarken, Berliner Designgrößen und internationalen Designerlabels, Accessoires, Kosmetik und Lifestylebüchern, sondern ist gleichzeitig eine Plattform für verschiedenste Events und Modepräsentationen.

F95 STORE is a must for trend-setters and fashionistas. This shopping mecca created by the people behind the renowned Premium Fashion Fair, held twice a year in Berlin, is open year-round to its loyal followers. F95 STORE has also a good range of modern jean labels by major Berlin designers as well as international designers, accessories, cosmetics, and practical books, and it is also a venue for different events and fashion parades.

INDEX

BILDNACHWEIS | PICTURE CREDITS l. left | r. right | b. below | a. above

© Mirela Abadi | Kaviar Gauche
Kate Bellm (110, 111, 130)

© Magdalena Barbe | Dawid Tomaszewski
Mina Gerngross (115 a.), Michal Martychowiec (114, 116, 117)

© Katrin Baumgart | Marcel Ostertag
Petra Dufkova (161)

© Fiona Bennett
Peter Hönnemann (181 a.), Sebastian Burgold (180)

Christine Anna Bierhals

1980 in Deutschland geboren, ist studierte Modedesignerin und Journalistin. Die Autorin von „City Fashion Berlin" ist heute als Modejournalistin und Stylistin international in der Modebranche tätig.

Born in Germany in 1980, Christine Anna Bierhals studied fashion design and journalism. The author of *City Fashion Berlin* works as a fashion journalist and stylist in the international sphere of the world of fashion.

City Fashion Berlin

© 2011 Tandem Verlag GmbH
h.f.ullmann is an imprint of Tandem Verlag GmbH

Text and concept: Christine Anna Bierhals
Layout and design: Laura Gerster | Mayolove
Co-authors: Melanie Leyendecker, Wolfgang Altmann
Map: DuMont Reisekartografie GmbH
Cover photo: © Sacha Tassilo Höchstetter
Cover creative director & styling: Christine Anna Bierhals
Cover design: Laura Gerster | Mayolove
Cover hair & make-up: Stefan Kehl
Cover model: Agnes Sokolowska
Cover location: CAFE MOSKAU, Berlin
Cover outfit: f.rau

Translation from German to English: Lynda Trevitt
English coordination and typesetting: Quality, Servicios Globales Editoriales, S.L.
Project management: Isabel Weiler
Overall responsibility for production: h.f.ullmann publishing, Potsdam, Germany

ISBN 978-3-8331-6062-2

Printed in China

10 9 8 7 6 5 4 3 2 1
X IX VIII VII VI V IV III II I

www.ullmann-publishing.com
newsletter@ullmann-publishing.com